# The Kurma Purana

DIPAVALI DEBROY
BIBEK DEBROY

# BOOKS FOR ALL
**Delhi-110052**

Distributed By:
**D K Publishers Distributors P Ltd.**
1, Ansari Road, Darya Ganj,
New Delhi-110002
Phones: 3278368, 3261465
Fax: 3264368
visit us at: www.dkpd.com
e-mail: dkpd@del3.vsnl.net.in

ISBN  81-7386-027-0 (Set)
        81-7386-042-4 (Vol.15)

**Published By:**
**Books For All**
B-2, Vardhaman Palace,
Nimri Commercial Centre,
Ashok Vihar Phase-IV,
Delhi-110052
Phone: 7401672, 7452453
visit us at: www.lppindia.com
e-mail: lpp@nde.vsnl.net.in

**Printed At:**
D K Fine Art Press P Ltd.
Delhi-110052

**PRINTED IN INDIA**

## Introduction

The *Kurma Purana* is the fifteenth *mahapurana*. But what exactly is a *mahapurana*? A *Purana* is a sacred text written many hundreds of years ago. In general, such a text will relate the stories and the religious rituals that form an important part of the beliefs of Hinduism. There are several such *Puranas*. Some of them are major ones and are referred to as *mahapuranas*. These are eighteen in number and were composed, or so scholars believe, between the years 300 A.D. and 1000 A.D. The *Kurma Purana* is one such text, and as you have just learnt, is listed fifteenth in the catalogue of *mahapuranas*. In addition, there are several minor *Puranas*, known as *upapuranas*. These were composed much later.

The time span 300 A.D. to 1000 A.D. is rather a long one. Why isn't it possible to date the composition of the *mahapuranas* more precisely? The reason is that the *Puranas* were not composed the way books are written today. Books today are usually written by a single author, at one point of time. But the *Puranas* developed their present forms in a different fashion. There may have been an original text. This spread by way of mouth, since writing was unknown. And at each recital, the reciter added his own compositions to what he himself had learnt. Thus the *Puranas* grew in volume, successively down through the ages. These later additions are known as interpolations. The problem is that, today it is impossible to decipher what was a later addition and what formed part of the original text. In this sense, the *mahapuranas* do not have a single author. Nor were they composed at any one particular point of time. Hence the broad range from 300 A.D. to 1000 A.D.

The traditional belief is however different. You must have heard of the two great epics, the *Ramayana* and the *Mahabharata*. The *Ramayana* is believed to have been composed by the sage Valmiki and the *Mahabharata* by the sage Vedavyasa (alternatively Vyasadeva). The traditional belief is that it was Vedavyasa who composed the eighteen *mahapuranas* after having composed the *Mahabharata*. The *Mahabharata* has one lakh *shlokas* or couplets. After composing the *Mahabharata*, Vedavyasa was apparently not quiet content with the stories that he had recounted in the epic. He therefore, composed the *mahapuranas*. The eighteen major *Puranas* have, between them, four lakh *shlokas*. Thus, Vedavyasa is believed to have composed five lakh couplets in all. But, as we have told you earlier, scholars do not subscribe to this belief.

The *mahapuranas* differ widely in length. The shortest is the *Markandeya Purana*. It has nine lakh couplets. The longest is the *Skanda Purana*, with eighty-one thousand couplets. The *Kurma Purana* has seventeen thousand couplets and is average in length.

Unfortunately, these couplets have not all survived. We know that the original *Kurma Purana* was divided into four sections or *samhitas*. Their names were *brahmi samhita*, *bhagavati samhita*, *souri samhita* and *vaishnavi samhita*. But the only section that is still available is the *brahmi samhita* and it is this which goes by the name of the *Kurma Purana* today. The *brahmi samhita* is divided into two parts (*bhaga*), a first part (*purva bhaga*) and an additional part (*upari bhaga*). The first part has fifty-two chapters (*adhyaya*) and the additional part has forty-four.

To be classified as a *mahapurana*, there are five characteristics (*lakshana*) that a text is required to exhibit. That is, there are five different subjects that the text must describe. These are the original creation of the universe (*sarga*), the periodical process of destruction and re-creation (*pratisarga*), the histories of the solar dynasty (*surya vamsha*) and lunar dynasty (*chandra vamsha*), royal genealogies (*vamshanucharita*) and the different eras (*manvantara*). As you will discover, the *Kurma Purana* does describe these five subjects.

You have probably heard of the sacred text that is known as the *Gita*. In the *Mahabharata*, the Kauravas and the Pandavas fought a battle on the plains of Kurukshetra. The *Gita* contains Krishna's teachings to Arjuna on the eve of the Kurukshetra battle. This, you are no doubt aware of, and you thus also know that the *Gita* is really a part of the *Mahabharata*. What you however probably do not know is the fact that there is more than one *Gita*. The text that is a part of the *Mahabharata* is not the only one of its kind. To distinguish it from other *Gitas*, one ought to refer to it by its complete name of *Shrimadbhagavata Gita*.

There is also a *Gita* that is part of the *Kurma Purana*. This is known as the *Ishvara Gita*. There is a technique of meditation known as *yoga*. This seeks to bring about an union between the human soul *(atman)* and the divine soul *(paramatman)*. The *Kurma Purana* itself will tell you more about *yoga*. *Yoga* is the primary subject matter of the *Shrimadbhagavata Gita*, as it is of the *Ishvara Gita*.

There is one particular way in which the eighteen *mahapuranas* are classified, although the division does seem to be slightly artificial. The Hindu Trinity consists of the gods Brahma, Vishnu and Shiva. Brahma is regarded as the creator, Vishnu as the preserver and Shiva as the destroyer. Since all three are important gods, any *Purana* will tend to extol and glorify all three. But there is often a difference in relative emphasis across the various *Puranas*. Those which describe the creation in great detail tend to glorify Brahma more and are known as *rajasika Puranas*. Those which devote a considerable part of the text to Vishnu's incarnations (*avatara*) tend to glorify Vishnu more and are known as *sattvika Puranas*. Texts which catalogue norms and rituals at great length tend to glorify Shiva more and are known as *tamasika Puranas*. The *Kurma Purana* is a *tamasika Purana*, together with five other *mahapuranas*. The remaining five are the *Matsya Purana*, the *Linga Purana*, the *Shiva Purana*, the *Skanda Purana* and the *Agni Purana*.

You have been told about the traditional belief that Vedavyasa composed the eighteen major *Puranas*. Who was this Vedavyasa? You must first realise that Vedavyasa is not a proper name, it is a title. The *Vedas* are sacred texts. When evil reigns on earth, the knowledge and wisdom of the *Vedas* is often lost and not properly disseminated amongst people. A sage then takes up the task of properly classifying the texts of the *Vedas*. In the process, he divides (*vyasa*) the *Vedas* and the title of Vedavyasa is conferred on him. It is believed that there have been twenty-eight Vedavyases to date and that there will be a twenty-ninth one before the world is destroyed. The Vedavyasa who is credited with having composed the *Mahabharata* and the *mahapuranas* was twenty-eighth in the list. His proper name was Krishna Dvaipayana and he was the son of Satyavati and the sage Parashara. The word *krishna* means dark and he was called Krishna because he was dark in complexion. The word *dvipa* means island and he obtained the name of Dvaipayana because he was born on an island.

Finally, a word about why the *Kurma Purana* is so named. The word *kurma* means turtle. The belief is that there have been several incarnations of Vishnu to date. Most *Puranas* state that there have been nine incarnations upto now. The second of these was as a turtle or *kurma*. It is in his form of a turtle that Vishnu recited the *Kurma Purana*. Hence the name.

Let us now get straight into what the *Purana* has to say.

## Lomaharshana and the Other Sages

There was a sage named Lomaharshana or Romaharshana. Vedavyasa was his *guru* (teacher) and Vedavyasa taught him the *Puranas*. This knowledge so thrilled *(harshita)* the student's body-hair *(roma* or *loma)* that he came to acquire the name of Lomaharshana or Romaharshana.

There was a forest named *naimisharanya* and several sages organised a sacrifice *(yajna)* in that forest. On the occasion of the sacrifice, they told Lomaharshana, "The great Vedavyasa has taught you the *Puranas*. There is no one as knowledgeable as you in these matters. Please recite to us the *Kurma Purana*."

"I will," replied Lomaharshana. "But first let me tell you the names of the eighteen *mahapuranas*.

They are *Brahma Purana*, *Padma Purana*, *Vishnu Purana*, *Shiva Purana*, *Bhagavata Purana*, *Bhavishya Purana*, *Narada Purana*, *Markandeya Purana*, *Agni Purana*, *Brahmavaivarta Purana*, *Linga Purana*, *Varaha Purana*, *Skanda Purana*, *Vamana Purana*, *Kurma Purana*, *Matsya Purana*, *Garuda Purana*, *Vayu Purana* and *Brahmanda Purana*. There are also eighteen *upapuranas*."

(This list will no doubt puzzle you. Haven't you been told that there are eighteen *mahapuranas*? Yet, if you go through Lomaharshana's list, you will find that there are nineteen *mahapuranas* listed - not eighteen. That there are eighteen major *Puranas* is accepted by all. But there is some disagreement about which texts are *mahapuranas* and which are not. More accurately, there is consensus about seventeen of the *mahapuranas*, the disagreement is about the eighteenth text in the list. In some cases, the *Shiva Purana* is listed. In other cases, it is the *Vayu Purana* that is so honoured. As it happens, both texts are mentioned by Lomaharshana. As for the *upapuranas*, there is disagreement about those as well. There is consensus about there being eighteen of them, but the names vary from one source to another.)

"From the list you can see that the *Kurma Purana* is the fifteenth *mahapurana*," continued Lomaharshana. "It has four sections - the *brahmi samhita*, the *bhagavati samhita*, the *souri samhita* and the *vaishnavi samhita*. There are six thousand *shlokas* in the *brahmi samhita*."

Many years ago, the gods *(devas)* and the demons *(danavas)* resolved to churn the ocean *(samudra manthana)* together. They were hopeful that the life-giving drink of *amrita* would emerge as a result of churning the ocean. The Mount Mandara was used as a churning rod. To provide a base for the mountain to rest on, the great Vishnu adopted the form of a turtle *(kurma)* and placed Mandara on his back. As a result of the churning of the ocean, Lakshmi, the goddess of wealth and prosperity, emerged and was united with Vishnu.

(The *samudra manthana* story is given in great detail in the *Ramayana* and the *Mahabharata.* As for Lakshmi, some of the *Puranas* state that she was born as the daughter of Khyati and the sage Bhrigu. She was then married to Vishnu. But the demons defeated the gods and Indra, as the king of the gods, lost his kingdoms. Lakshmi, the goddess of wealth and prosperity, deserted Indra. The sage Durvasa therefore cursed Lakshmi that she would have to live in the ocean. And when the ocean was churned, Lakshmi emerged yet again.)

Indra, the other gods, and the sages were charmed at Lakshmi's beauty when she appeared. "Who is this wonderful goddess?" they asked Vishnu.

"This is Lakshmi," replied Vishnu. "She is also known as Shakti. It is with her help that I delude the universe and its inhabitants with my illusions *(maya)*. It is Lakshmi who gives me all my powers, although she is no different from me in essence."

Vishnu then proceeded to tell the gods and the sages the story of Indradyumna.

## Indradyumna

Many years ago, there was a king named Indradyumna. He ruled the world well and, when he died, was reborn as a *brahmana*. (The *brahmanas* constitute the first of the four classes, their primary duties are to study the *Vedas* and perform sacrifices.)

As a *brahmana*, Indradyumna observed religious rites and meditated. He also started to pray to the goddess Lakshmi. When Lakshmi appeared, Indradyumna begged of her, "Please tell me about yourself. Please give me insight into what constitutes true knowledge."

"Even the gods and the sages are unable to comprehend my true nature," replied Lakshmi. "I am Vishnu's illusions and there is no difference between him and me. As for knowledge, it is beyond my powers to grant you that. You will have to pray to the great Vishnu himself."

Having said this, Lakshmi disappeared, and Indradyumna started to pray to Vishnu. Several years passed, but Indradyumna continued to meditate. Finally, Vishnu appeared and instructed Indradyumna on the path to true knowledge.

"What did you tell Indradyumna?" asked the gods and the sages. "What was this wonderful knowledge?"

"I will repeat it for your benefit," replied Vishnu.

Since Vishnu repeated his teachings while in the form of a turtle or *Kurma*, these sacred words are known as the *Kurma Purana*. There are many subjects that Vishnu's instructions covered, but let us first start with the concept of *varnashrama dharma*. *Dharma* means righteousness and these precepts lay down the fundamental principles of righteous conduct. This is typified in the system of four *varnas* (classes) and four *ashramas* (stages of life).

## Varnashrama Dharma

Vishnu said that before creation began, there was only water in the universe and Vishnu slept on these waters. When it was time for creation to begin, Brahma emerged from Vishnu's body. And Shiva emerged from Vishnu's anger. Lakshmi too was created from Vishnu's body and took her place by Vishnu's side.

Brahma told Vishnu, "Please use this goddess to delude the beings whom I will create. Tell her to sow the seeds of illusions in their minds. Please tell her to make the righteous prosper."

Vishnu complied. He requested Lakshmi, "Please delude and destroy gods, demons and humans who are about to be created. But please leave the righteous alone and make them prosper. I will tell you how to know the righteous. They are those that follow the precepts of *varnashrama dharma*."

The *brahmanas* constitute the first of the four classes. Brahma created nine sons from his mental powers. Their names were Marichi, Bhrigu, Angira, Pulastya, Pulaha, Kratu, Daksha, Atri and Vashishtha. These sons became sages and they were the first *brahmanas*. They were created from Brahma's mouth. There are six types of action that are recommended for *brahmanas*. These are *yajana* (performing sacrifices), *yajana* (acting as priests at sacrifices), *dana* (donation of alms), *pratigraha* (receiving gifts), *adhyapana* (teaching) and *adhyayana* (studying). A *brahmana* who performs these tasks well, attains the wonderful place known as *prajapatya*. (This would seem to be synonymous with Brahma's residence of Brahmaloka.)

The *kshatriyas* constitute the second of the four classes. They were created from Brahma's arms. The duties of *kshatriyas* include *dana* (donation of alms), *adhyayana* (studying) and performing *yajnas* (sacrifices). But their primary duties are to take up arms and fight. It is their job to punish the evil and protect the good. A *kshatriya* who performs these tasks well, attains Indra's residence of Indraloka.

The *vaishyas* constitute the third of the four classes. They were created from Brahma's thighs. Like the *kshatriyas*, the *vaishyas* can also donate alms, study and perform sacrifices. But their primary duty is agriculture. (In many other *Puranas*, trade and animal husbandry are mentioned in additon to agriculture.) A *vaishya* who performs these tasks well, gets to live with Vayu, the god of the wind.

The *shudras* constitute the last of the four classes. They were created from Brahma's feet. Their primary duty is to serve the other three classes. In addition, a *shudra* can adopt artisanship as an occupation. A *shudra* who performs these tasks well, will live with the *gandharvas* (singers of heaven).

Generally speaking, all four classes have to observe the religion that is prescribed in the *Vedas*. There are various other *shastras* (religious texts) that circulate on earth. But many of them are against the *Vedas*. The religion that is prescribed in such anti-Vedic texts must not be followed. Only sinners follow such religions, and they are doomed to eternal damnation.

There are four *ashramas* (stages of life). The first one is *brahmacharya* (celibate studenthood). The primary duties of a person who is in this stage of life are studying the *Vedas* and serving one's *guru* (teacher) well. He has to live on alms that are obtained through begging. When this stage of life is over, there are two options that are available to the individual. In rare instances, he may desire to devote the rest of his life to studying and meditation. Such a person is known as *naishthika*. More commonly, individuals wish to step into the next stage of life. An individual who does so is known as an *upakurvana*.

The second stage of life is *garhasthya* (householder stage). A householder's primary duties are serving guests, performing sacrifices, donating alms, worshipping the gods and keeping the sacred fire burning in the house at all times. In cases where the householder is absent from the house, these functions are to be performed by his wife or sons, or even by his priest. A householder must not also forget to study a little bit of the *Vedas* every day. The householder stage is superior to the other three stages of life. The reason is that the alms provided by a householder are the means of sustenance for individuals who are in the other three stages of life. A householder may be one of two types. He may be a *sadhaka*, in which case his chief obsession is that of satisfying his friends and relatives. Alternatively, there may be a householder who is *udasina*. This means that he is not really interested in his wife, his sons or in the acquisition of material wealth. His chief obsession is that of being freed from the bonds of the world.

The third stage of life is *vanaprastha* (forest-dwelling stage). Such a person retires to the forest and lives on fruits and roots. He studies the *Vedas*, performs *tapasya* (meditation) and observes religious rites. But one should never embark on a forest-dwelling stage unless one's mind is ready for it. This also means that one must have had sons. Without sons to carry on the line, it is not recommended that a householder venture out on the forest-dwelling stage. There are two types of forest-dwellers. The first type consists of individuals who primarily devote themselves to worshipping the gods and performing religious ceremonies. Such an individual is known as a *tapasa*, because he does do some *tapasya*. But there are individuals who devote themselves entirely to meditation. Such a person is known as a *sannyasika*, since there is very little of difference between him and a *sannyasi* (hermit).

The fourth and final stage of life is *sannyasa* (hermithood). Such individuals spend all their time in meditating. They beg food for a living. It is not proper to become a hermit unless one's mind has achieved detachment from the world. There are two types of hermits. The first type consists of those who are trying to realise the true nature of the *atman* (human soul). such a person treats all other individuals as he would treat himself and is known as a *yogi*. But there are also hermits who go through intense meditation so as to attain the supreme wisdom. Such a person is known as a *parameshthika*.

There are various other traits that are demanded by the righteous way of life. One must forgive and display pity, one must not be jealous and must be ready to sacrifice one's own selfish interests. One must be truthful, practise non-violence and learn to control the senses. One must also visit *tirthas* (places of pilgrimage). It is also important to realise that one does not perform actions for the sake of the fruits of the actions. The fruits of all actions vest with the *brahman* (the divine essence). In fact, it is a gross misconception to think that a specific action is being performed by an individual. All actions are performed by the *brahman*, the ordinary human being is merely an instrument. As long as this realisation is missing, an individual is ignorant and is doomed to the shackles of worldly bonds.

## Creation

Vishnu next narrated to the gods and the sages the history of creation.

In the beginning, the *brahman* was everywhere. The *brahman* had no form, but nor was it without form. It had no beginning and no end. It had no traits, but nor was it without traits. The *brahman* is impossible to describe, sense or see.

Brahma, Vishnu and Shiva are derived from the *brahman*. Brahma performs the function of a creator, Vishnu that of a preserver and Shiva that of a destroyer.

When it was time for creation to begin, the *brahman* created water throughout the universe. Before that, there was nothing. In the water, there appeared a golden *(hiranya)* egg *(anda)*. The egg grew in size and Brahma, the creator, appeared inside the egg. Everything that there is in the universe, was already there, in embryonic form, inside the egg. There were gods, the demons, humans, the sun, the moon, the stars, the planets and the wind. The word *garbha* means womb and since Brahma originated from inside a golden (hiranya) egg, he is known as Hiranyagarbha. Brahma was the first being to be created. He had four faces. He had no birth (janana) in the real sense of the term. He is therefore also referred to as Aja (without birth). It is also true that he created (bhuva) himself (svayam). It is because of this that Brahma is known as Svayambhu. Brahma was to be the lord (pati) of all the subjects who were going to be born (praja). Thus, Brahma acquired the name of Prajapati.

To appreciate how creation took place, it is first necessary to have some conception about the nature of time.

## A Digression on Time

The smallest unit of time is a nimesha. Fifteen nimeshas make one kashtha, thirty kashthas are one kala and thirty kalas constitute one muhurta. There are thirty muhurtas in a span of day and night (ahoratra). Thirty such ahoratras make up a month. There are two pakshas (fornight) in every month. Six months constitute an ayana and two ayanas a year. There are thus twelve months in every year. The names of the two ayanas are uttarayana and dakshinayana. While humans pass through uttarayana, the gods pass through only one day. Similarly, when humans pass through dakshinayana, the gods pass through merely one night. One year for humans is equivalent to a time span of one day and one night for the gods.

Twelve thousand years of the gods make up one *mahayuga*. This is subdivided into four *yugas* (eras). The names of these eras are *satya yuga* or *krita yuga*, *treta yuga*, *dvapara yuga* and *kali yuga*. *Satya yuga* has four thousand years, *treta yuga* three thousand, *dvapara yuga* two thousand and *kali yuga* one thousand. This adds up to ten thousand years. But there are also periods that join two *yugas*: (*sandhyamsha*). *Satya yuga* has a *sandhyamsha* of four hundred years, *treta yuga* of three hundred, *dvapara yuga* of two hundred and *kali yuga* of one hundred. There will therefore be seven hundred additional years between *satya yuga* and *treta yuga*, five hundred between *treta yuga* and *dvapara yuga*, three hundred between *dvapara yuga* and *kali yuga* and five hundred between *kali yuga* and the next *satya yuga*. These are two thousand additional years, and when added up to the earlier figure of ten thousand, make up twelve thousand years.

There are a little over seventy-one *manvantaras* (eras) in each *mahayuga*. Each *manvantara* is a time period that is ruled over by a Manu. The first Manu in the present *kalpa* (cycle) was Svayambhuva Manu and there were several other Manus after him. Each *kalpa* in fact passes during one of Brahma's days and there are fourteen *manvantaras* in a *kalpa*. Stated differently, there are one thousand *mahayugas* in every *kalpa*.

Three hundred and sixty *kalpas* constitute one of Brahma's years. One hundred times this time period is known as a *parardha*. At the end of this period, the whole universe is destroyed and Brahma, Vishnu and Shiva are also destroyed. At the end of the destruction, creation starts afresh and this creation is known as *sarga*.

There is a smaller process of destruction that takes place at the end of every *kalpa*. Brahma, Vishnu and Shiva are not destroyed, but everything else is. The creation that comes at the end of this minor destruction is known as *pratisarga*.

The present *kalpa* is known as *varaha kalpa*. The one that preceded it was known as *padma kalpa*.

"Why is the present *kalpa* called *varaha kalpa*?" the gods and the sages asked Vishnu.

Vishnu told them the story of his boar incarnation.

**The Boar Incarnation**

A *varaha* is a boar and the boar incarnation is usually catalogued as the third of Vishnu's ten incarnations.

When the universe was submerged in water after the destruction that came at the end of *padma kalpa*, Vishnu slept on the waters. Thus he slept for a thousand *mahayugas*. Since the word *nara* means water and *ayana* means resting-place, Vishnu is also referred to as Narayana.

Brahma decided to start creation afresh, but discovered that the earth was submerged in water. How would his creations survive if there was no earth? He therefore requested Vishnu to bring the earth up from under the water.

Vishnu adopted the form of a boar and went to the underworld. He discovered the earth there and raised her up on the tusks of the boar. The boar carefully raised the earth and laid her to rest on top of the water. The earth began to float like a gigantic boat.

Since Vishnu raised the earth in the form of a boar at the beginning of the *kalpa*, the present cycle is known as *varaha kalpa*.

(The story of the boar incarnation is rather summarily disposed of in the *Kurma Purana*. The other *Puranas* describe it at great length. Apart from the question of raising up the earth from under the water, the story revolves around the demon Hiranyaksha. This demon was the son of the sage Kashyapa and his wife Diti. He defeated the gods and drove them out of heaven. In desperation, the gods started to pray to Vishnu. Hiranyaksha used to live under the water and Vishnu entered the water in his form of a boar and killed Hiranyaksha. He also recovered the *Vedas* which had been stolen by Hiranyaksha.)

**Creation Continued**

Brahma first created five sons through his mental powers. Their names were Sanaka,

Sanatana, Sanandana, Kratu and Sanatakumara. These five sons became sages and did not have any offspring. Brahma therefore had to create some more beings so that the population of the universe might increase. But prior to that, he decided to perform *tapasya*. However, the meditation did not yield him any results and Brahma became very angry and disheartened. He started to weep and a teardrop fell on the ground. From this drop, there emerged Shiva.

Brahma bowed before Shiva and said, "Please create some living beings."

This Shiva proceeded to do. But all the beings that Shiva created were mirror images of himself. That is, they were all immortal.

"What are you doing?" exclaimed Brahma. "Stop creating these immortals. Create mortal beings. Create those who will suffer from old age and will die."

"I beg your pardon," retorted Shiva. "That I refuse to do. Old age and disease are not objects that should be sought after. In fact, they are evil. I flatly refuse to create such evil."

"All right then," said Brahma, "I will take care of creation myself. Please stop creating."

The first objects that Brahma created were water, fire, the sky, heaven *(svarga)*, wind, rivers, mountains, oceans, trees, herbs and time.

Brahma next created eleven sons from his mental powers. Their names were Marichi, Bhrigu, Angira, Pulastya, Pulaha, Kratu, Daksha, Atri, Vashishtha, Dharma and Sankalpa.

(In the earlier section on *varnashrama dharma*, only nine sons were mentioned. Dharma and Sankalpa did not figure in that list.)

Thereafter, Brahma created four classes of beings. These were gods, demons, ancestors *(pitris)* and humans. The demons were born from Brahma's thighs, the gods from his mouth. The snakes *(sarpa)*, the *yakshas* (demi-gods), the ghosts *(bhuta)* and the *gandharvas* were born next. Cows were born from Brahma's stomach, and horses, elephants, donkeys, deer, camels and mules from his feet. Herbs and trees emerged from Brahma's body-hair.

(This account contradicts a more common account given in some of the other *Puranas*, such as the *Bhagavata Purana.* In the more usual account, all beings are descended from the sage Kashyapa. Kashyapa married thirteen of Daksha's daughters. These daughters were named Aditi, Diti, Danu, Kashtha, Arishtha. Surasa, Ila, Muni, Krodhavasha, Tamra, Surabhi, Sarama and Timi. Aditi's offspring were the gods *(adityas)*, Diti's the demons *(daityas)*. Danu's offspring were other demons *(danavas)*, Kashtha's children horses, Arishtha's *gandharvas*, Surasa's demons *(rakshasas)*, Ila's offspring trees and herbs, Muni's the *apsaras* (dancers of heaven), Krodhavasha's ghosts (pishachas), Tamra's birds, Surabhi's cattle, Sarama's wild animals and Timi's marine creatures. The Kurma Purana itself refers to this alternative account subsequently.)

To return to the present account of the Kurma Purana, Brahma thereafter divided his body into two. One half was male and was called Svayambhuva Manu. The remaining half was female and was called Shatarupa. Manu and Shatarupa married and had two sons and two daughters. The sons were named Priyavrata and Uttanapada and the daughters were named Prasuti and Akuti. Since all humans are Manu's descendants, they are known as manava.

Prasuti married Daksha and they had twenty-four daughters. (The Puranas are not at all consistent about the number of daughters Prasuti and Daksha had. The number is sometimes twenty-four, sometimes fifty and sometimes sixty.) Thirteen of the twenty-four daughters were married to Brahma's son Dharma. Of the remaining eleven, Khyati was married to Bhrigu, Sati to Shiva, Sambhuti to Marichi, Smriti to Angira, Priti to Pulastya, Kshama to Pulaha, Sannati to Kratu, Anasuya to Atri, Urjja to Vashishtha, Svaha to the fire-god Agni and Svadha to the ancestors (pitris).

## Brahma, Vishnu and Shiva

The gods and the sages told Vishnu, "We are getting a bit confused. You have told us that Brahma emerged from Vishnu's body. And yet you have also told us how Brahma was born inside a golden egg. Which of these is the correct account? Then again, you have told us that Shiva was born from one of Brahma's tears. But we have sometimes heard otherwise. Which is right? Please remove this confusion."

"There is no confusion," replied Vishnu. "Let me explain it for you."

Brahma was born from the golden egg right at the beginning, at the time of the original creation. But at the end of every *kalpa* there is a minor destruction when all living beings other than Brahma, Vishnu and Shiva die. When the destruction is over, creation has to start afresh.

At the end of the last *kalpa*, there was water everywhere in the universe. The heaven, the earth and the underworld, were all flooded with water. There were no gods and no sages. Only the great Vishnu slept on the water. He had a thousand hoods, a thousand eyes, a thousand arms and a thousand feet. This was his form of Ananta, the snake *(naga)*.

(The *Kurma Purana* completely identifies Vishnu with Ananta. More commonly, the *Puranas* state that the snake Ananta was the son of Kadru and the sage Kashyapa. He pleased Brahma through his prayers and obtained from Brahma the boon that he would be permitted to hold up the earth on his hoods. The *Kalika Purana* specifically states that, at the time of destruction, Vishnu and

Lakshmi rest on Ananta's central hood. The *Vishnu Purana* adds the information that Ananta was one of Balarama's *avataras*. The names Shesha, Vasuki and Gonasa are often used synonymously with Ananta.)

While Vishnu thus slept on the water, a wonderful lotus sprouted from his navel. The lotus was gigantic and shone like the sun. Its fragrance spread in all directions. Brahma appeared inside the lotus. Since *padma* means lotus and *yoni* means place of birth, Brahma is also known as Padmayoni.

Brahma saw Vishnu sleeping on the water and woke him up. "Who are you?" asked Brahma.

"I am Vishnu," replied Vishnu. "I am the origin of everything. But who are you ?"

"I am Brahma," was the answer. "I am the creator. Everything that will be there in the universe is inside my body."

"Is that really so?" asked Vishnu. "Let me see."

Vishnu thereupon entered Brahma's body. He really found the three worlds, the gods, the demons and the humans inside Brahma's stomach and was greatly surprised. He emerged from Brahma's mouth and told Brahma, "What I have seen inside your body is truly wonderful. But I too can show you many worlds inside my body. Please enter and see for yourself."

It was now Brahma's turn to enter Vishnu's body. But when Brahma did this, he could find no end to Vishnu's stomach. It was true that there were many worlds inside Vishnu's body. However, Brahma could find no way of coming out from Vishnu's stomach. He finally had to emerge through Vishnu's navel, through the stalk of the lotus that was there.

"How dare you try to confine me inside your body?" demanded Brahma, as soon as he managed to get out.

"Please do not get angry," replied Vishnu. "I merely thought that I would play with you for a while. Otherwise, it is inconceivable that anyone should dare to confine the great Brahma. Please pardon me. And as a token of your pardon, please grant me the boon that henceforth, you will be known as my son. After all, you did emerge from a lotus that grew out of my navel."

"Agreed," said Brahma. "Let us make peace. After all, there is no one else. We are the lords of everything, we are parts of the *brahman*."

"Please do not forget Shiva," responded Vishnu. "Your words will anger him and bring about your undoing."

While the two were thus conversing, Shiva appeared on the scene. He had a third eye in the middle of his forehead and his hair was matted. A trident could be seen in his hand.

"Who is this fellow?" asked Brahma. "He looks like an upstart."

Vishnu calmed Brahma down. He also gave Brahma divine eyes so that Brahma could comprehend the true nature of Shiva. Brahma then started to pray to Shiva. Pleased with Brahma's prayers, Shiva agreed to grant Brahma a boon.

"Please grant me the boon that you will be born as my son," said Brahma.

Shiva agreed to do so and went away.

### Rudra

Brahma returned to his seat on the lotus flower.

Suddenly, two demons named Madhu and Kaitabha appeared. They were exceedingly strong and threatened to destroy everything that Brahma would create. Brahma therefore requested Vishnu to kill these two demons. Vishnu created two beings from his own body and these two beings killed the demons.

(The Madhu and Kaitabha story is given in greater detail in other *Puranas*, such as the *Kalika Purana*. While Vishnu was sleeping, the two demons were born from his ears. One of them desired to have some honey as soon as he was born. Since the word for honey is *madhu*, he came to be known as Madhu. The other one looked like an insect. Since the word for insect is *kita*, he came to be known as Kaitabha. These brothers attacked Brahma and Vishnu had to fight with them so as to rescue Brahma. The fight went on for five thousand years before Vishnu could kill them. After the demons were killed, the fat (meda) from their bodies formed the earth. That is the reason why the earth is known as medini.)

After Madhu and Kaitabha had been killed, Brahma could start to create. He first created, through his mental powers, the sons whose names have earlier been mentioned. Since Shiva had promised that he would be born as Brahma's son, Brahma decided to perform tapasya so as to accomplish this. He prayed for many years, but nothing happened. In utter frustration, Brahma began to cry. The ghosts (bhuta and preta) were born from these tears. Brahma was so disgusted at having created these awful creatures, that he committed suicide. It was then that Shiva was born from Brahma's mouth and Brahma revived.

(You will have noticed the contradiction. Earlier, it had been stated that Shiva was born from a teardrop and there had been no mention of Brahma's suicide. The suicide is not mentioned in other Puranas either, nor is there any mention of Shiva or Rudra being born from a teardrop. In the Vishnu Purana, he suddenly appeared in Brahma's lap. In the Padma Purana, he was born from Brahma's furrowed brows.)

The baby started to cry as soon as he was born.

"Don't cry," said Brahma. "Since you cried when you were born, you will be known as Rudra."

(The *Kurma Purana* is not specific on why the baby cried. The other *Puranas* state that the baby cried for the want of a name. Brahma therefore gave the boy the name of Rudra, as the word *rud* means to cry. The boy continued to cry and Brahma gave him several other names as well. The *Puranas* however disagree about what these various names were.)

In addition to Rudra, Brahma gave the boy the names Bhava, Sarva, Ishana, Pashupati, Bhima, Ugra and Mahadeva. In these eight different forms, Shiva was to live in the sun, the water, the sky, the fire, the wind, the trees, the bodies of *brahmanas* and the moon.

## Parvati's Thousand Names

Shiva was married to Daksha's daughter Sati. Sati died and was reborn as Parvati, the daughter of Himalaya and his wife Mena (alternatively, Menaka). Parvati was married to Shiva.

In fact, Himalaya and Mena prayed so that they might have the goddess as their daughter. Pleased with their prayers, the goddess arrived before Himalaya and Mena and showed them her divine form. She also promised them that she would be born as their daughter.

There were a thousand names of the goddess that Himalaya recited in the course of his prayers (one thousand and eight to be precise). These names are as follows. For convenience, we have reproduced them in groups of ten names each.

(1) Shiva, Uma, Paramashakti, Ananta, Nishkala, Amala, Shanta, Maheshvari, Nitya, Shashvati.

(2) Paramakshara, Achintya, Kevala, Shivatma, Paramatma, Anadi, Avyaya, Shuddha, Devatma, Sarvaga.

(3) Achala, Eka, Anekavibhagastha, Mayatita, Sunirmala, Mahamaheshvari, Satya, Mahadevi, Niranjana, Kashtha.

(4) Sarvantarastha, Chitshakti, Atilalasa, Nanda, Sarvvatmika, Vidya, Jyotirupa, Amrita, Akshara, Shanti.

(5) Sarvvapratishtha, Nivritti, Amritaprada, Vyomamurti, Vyomalaya, Vyomadhara, Achyuta, Amara, Anadinidhana, Amogha.

(6) Karanatma, Kalakula, Svatahprathamaja, Amritanabhi, Atmasamshraya, Praneshvarapriya, Mata, Mahamahishaghatini, Pranarupa, Pradhana-purusheshvari.

(7) Sarvvashakti, Kalakara, Jyotsna, Sarvvakaryaniyantri, Sarvvabhuteshvari, Samsara-yoni, Sakala, Sarvvashaktisamudbhava, Samsar-apota, Durvara.

(8) Durnirikshya, Durasada, Pranashakti, Pranavidya, Yogini, Paramakala, Mahavibhuti, Durddharsha, Mulaprakritidsambhava.

(9) Anadyanantavitava, Paramaghapakarshini, Svargasthityantarakarani, Sudurvvachya, Duratyaya, Shabdayoni, Shabdamayi, Nadakhya, Nadavigraha, Anadi.

(10) Avyaktaguna, Mahananda, Sanatani, Akashayoni, Yogastha, Mahayogeshvareshvari, Mahamaya, Sudushpara, Mulaprakriti, Ishvari.

(11) Pradhanapurushatita, Pradhanapurushatmika, Purana, Chinmayi; Adipuruṣharupini, Bhutantavastha, Kutastha, Mahapurushasamjnita, Janmamrityujaratita, Sarvvashaktisamanvita.

(12) Vyapini, Anavachhinna, Pradhananupraveshini, Kshetrajnashakti, Avyaktalakshana, Malavarjjita, Anadimayasambinna, Prakritigraha, Mahamayasamutpanna, Tamasi.

(13) Pourushi, Dhruva, Vyaktatmika, Krishna, Avyaktatmika, Rakta, Shukla, Prasutika, Akarya, Karyajanani.

(14) Nityaprasavadharmini, Sargapralayanirmukta, Srishtisthityantadharmini, Brahmagarbha, Chaturvimsha, Padmanabha, Achyutatmika, Vaidyuti, Shashvati, Yoni.

(15) Jaganmata, Ishvarapriya, Sarvvadhara, Maharupa, Sarvvaisharyasamannita, Vishvarupa, Mahagarbha, Vishveshechhanuvartini, Mahiyasi, Brahmayoni.

(16) Mahalakshmisamudbhava, Mahavimanamadhyastha, Mahanidra, Atmahetuka, Sarvva-

sadharani, Sukshma, Avidya, Paramarthiki, Anantarupa, Anantastha.

(17) Purushamohini, Devi, Anekakarasa-msthana, Kalatrayavivarjita, Brahmajanma, Harimurti, Brahmakhya, Brahmavishnu-shivatmika, Brahmeshavishnujanani, Brahma-samshraya.

(18) Vyakta, Prathamaja, Brahmi, Mahati, Brahmarupini, Vairagyaishvaryadharmatma, Brahmamurti, Hridisthita, Apamyoni, Svayam-bhuti.

(19) Manasi, Tattvasambhava, Ishvarani, Sarvvani, Shankararddhasharirini, Bhavani, Rudrani, Mahalakshmi, Ambika, Maheshvara-samutpanna.

(20) Bhuktimuktifalaprada, Sarvveshvari, Sarvvavandya, Nitamuditamanasa, Brahmendro-pendranamita, Shankarechhanuvartini, Ishvararddhasanagata, Maheshvarapativrata, Sakridvibhata, Sarvvartisamudraparishoshini.

(21) Parvati, Himavatputri, Paramanandadayini, Gunadhya, Yogaja, Yogya, Jnanamurti, Vikashini, Savitri, Kamala.

(22) Lakshmi, Shri, Anantavakshahsthalasthita, Sarojanilaya, Ganga, Yoganidra, Asurardini Sarasvati, Sarvvavidya, Jagajjveyashtha.

(23) Sumangala, Vagdevi Varada, Avachya Kirti, Sarvvarthasadhika, Yogishvari, Brahmavidya, Mahavidya, Sushobhana.

(24) Guhyavidya, Atmavidya, Dharmavidya, Atmabhavita, Svaha, Vishvambhara, Siddhi, Svadha, Medha, Dhriti.

(25) Shruti, Niti, Suniti, Sukriti, Madhavi, Naravahini, Pujya, Vibhavati, Soumya, Bhogini.

(26) Bhogashayini, Shobha, Vamshakari, Lola, Manini, Parameshthini, Trailokyasundari, Ramya, Sundari, Kamacharini.

(27) Mahanubhava, Sattvastha, Mahamahisha-mardini, Padmamala, Papahara, Vichitramukutan-gada, Kanta, Chitrambaradhara, Divyabharana-bhushita.

(28) Hamsakhya, Vyomanilaya, Jagasrishtivivar-ddhini, Niyantri, Yantramadhyastha, Nandini, Bhadrakalika, Adityavarna, Koumari.

(29) Mayuravaravahana, Vrishasanagata, Gouri, Mahakali, Surarchita Aditi, Niyata, Roudri, Padmagarbhavivahana.

(30) Virupakshi, Lelihana, Mahasuravinashini, Mahafala, Anavadyangi, Kamarupa, Vibhavari, Koushiki, Vichitraratnamukuta, Pranatarti-prabhanjani.

(31) Karshani, Ratri, Tridashartivinashini, Vahurupa, Virupa, Surupa, Rupavarjita, Bhaktartishamani, Bhavya, Bhavatapavinashini.

(32) Nirguna, Nityavibhava, Nihsara, Nirapa-trapa, Tapasvini, Samagiti, Bhavankanilayalaya, Diksha, Vidyadhari, Dipta.

(33) Manendrarinipatini, Sarvvatishayini, Vidya, Sarvvasiddhipradayini, Sarvveshvarapriya, Tarkshi, Samudrantaravasini, Akalanka, Niradhara.

(34) Nityasiddha, Niramaya, Kamadhenu, Vrihadgarbha, Dhimati, Mohanashini, Nihsankalpa, Niratanka, Vinaya.

(35) Vinayapriya, Jvalamalasahasradhya, Devadevi, Manomayi, Mahabhagavati, Bhaga, Vasudevasamudbhava, Mahendrapendrabhagini.

(36) Bhaktigamya, Paravara, Jnanajneya, Jaratita, Vedantavishaya, Gati, Dakshina, Dahana, Danta, Sarvvabhutanamaskrita.

(37) Yogamaya, Vibhagajna, Mahamoha, Gariyasi, Sandhya, Brahmavidyashraya, Vijankurasamudhbuti, Mahashakti, Mahamati, Kshanti.

(38) Prajna, Chiti, Samvit, Mahabhogindra-shayini, Vikriti, Shankari, Shanti, Ganagandharvasevita, Vaishvanari, Mahashala.

(39) Devasena, Guhapriya, Maharatri, Shivananda, Shachi, Duhsvapnanashini, Ijya, Pujya, Jagaddhatri, Durvineya.

(40) Surpini, Guhalvika, Gunotpatti, Mahapitha, Marutsuta, Havyavahantaragadi, Havyavahasa-mudhbhava, Jagadyoni, Jaganmata, Janma-mrityujaratiga.

(41) Vuddhi, Mahavuddhimati, Purushantara-vasini, Tarasvini, Samadhistha, Trinetra, Divisamsthita, Sarvvendriyamanomata, Sarvva-bhutahridisthita, Samsaratarini.

(42) Brahmavadimanolaya, Brahmani, Vrihati, Brahmi, Brahmabhuta, Bhavarani, Hiranmayi, Maharatri, Samsaraparivartika, Sumalini.

(43) Surupa, Bhavini, Harini, Prabha, Unmilani, Sarvasaha, Sarvvapratyayasakshini, Susoumya, Chandravadana, Tandavasaktamanasa.

(44) Sattvashuddhikari, Shuddhi, Malatraya-vinashini, Jagatpriya, Jaganmurti, Trimurti, Amritashraya, Nirashraya, Nirahara, Nirankushapadodbhava.

(45) Chakrahasta, Vichitrangi, Sragvini, Padmadharini, Paravaravidhanajna, Maha-purushapurvaja, Vishveshvarapriya, Vidyut, Vidyujjihva, Jitashrama.

(46) Vidyamayi, Sahasrakshi, Sahasrava-danatmaja, Sahasrarashmi, Sattvastha, Maheshvarapadashraya, Kshalini, Mrinmayi, Vyapta, Padmavodhika.

(47) Taijasi, Mahamayashraya, Manya, Mahadevamanorama, Vyomalakshmi, Simharatha, Chekitana, Amitaprabha, Vireshvari, Vimanastha.

(48) Vishoka, Shokanashini, Anahata, Kundalini, Nalini, Padmabhasini, Sadananda, Sadakirti, Vagdevata, Sarvvabhutashrayasthita.

(49) Brahmakala, Vishnushivagraja, Paragati, Kshobhika, Bandhika, Bhedya, Bhedabheda-vivarjita, Kalalita, Kalarani.

(50) Brahmashri, Brahmahridaya, Vyomashakti, Kriyashakti, Janashakti, Abhinna, Bhinnasamsthana, Vashini, Vamshakarini, Guhyashakti.

(51) Gunatita, Sarvada, Sarvatomukhi, Bhagini, Bhagavatpatni, Sakala, Kalakarini, Sarvvavit, Sarvvatobhadra.

(52) Guhyatita, Guharani, Prakriya, Yogamata, Ganga, Vishveshareshvari, Kapila, Akapila, Kanta, Kamalabha.

(53) Kalantara, Punya, Pushkarini, Bhoktri, Purandarapurahsara, Poshani, Paramaishvarya-bhutida, Bhutibhushana, Panchabrahmasa-mutpatti.

(54) Paramarthavigraha, Dharmodaya, Bha-numati, Yogijneya, Manojava, Manorama, Mano-raska, Tapasi, Vedarupini, Vedashakti.

(55) Vedamata, Vedavidyaprakashini, Yogesh-vareshvari, Mata, Mahashakti, Manomayi, Vishvavastha, Viyanmurti, Vidyunmala, Vihayasi.

(56) Kinnari, Surabhi, Vidya, Nandini, Nandivallabha, Bharati, Paramananda, Parapara-vibhedika, Sarvvapraharanopeta, Kamya.

(57) Kameshvareshvari, Achintya, Ananta-vibhava, Bhulekha, Kanakaprabha, Kushmandi,

Dhanaratnadhya, Sugandha, Gandhadayini, Trivikramapadodbhuta.

(58) Dhanushpani, Shivodaya, Sudurlabha, Dhanadhyaksha, Dhanya, Pingalalochana, Shanti, Prabhavati, Dipti, Pankajayatalochana.

(59) Adya, Hritkamalodbhuta, Gomata, Ranapriya, Satkriya, Girisha, Shuddhi, Nityapushta, Nirantara, Durga.

(60) Katyayani, Chandi, Charichitanga, Suvigraha, Hiranyavarna, Jagati, Jagadyantra-pravartika, Sarada, Mandaradrinivasa, Svarnamalini.

(61) Ratnamala, Ratnagarbha, Pushti, Vishvapramathini, Padmanana, Padmanibha, Ni-tyatushta, Amritodbhava, Dhunvati, Dushpra-kampa.

(62) Suryamata, Drishadvati, Mahendrabhagini, Soumya, Varenya, Varadayika, Kalyani, Kamalavasa, Panchachuda, Varaprada.

(63) Vachya, Amareshvari, Vandya, Durjjaya, Duratikrama, Kalaratri, Mahabega, Virabhadrapriya, Hita, Bhadrakali.

(64) Jaganmata, Bhaktamangaladayini, Karala, Pingalakara, Kamabheda, Mahasvana, Yashasvini, Yashoda, Shadadhvaparivartika, Shankhini.

(65) Padmini, Sankhya, Samkhyayogapravartika, Chaitra, Samvatsararuda, Jagatsampurani, Indraja, Shumbhari, Khechari, Khastha.

(66) Kambugriva, Kalipriya, Khagadhvaja, Khagaruda, Varahi, Pugamalini, Aishvaryapadmanilaya, Virakta, Garudasana, Jayanti.

(67) Hridguhagamya, Shankareshtaganagrani, Samyastha, Sankalpasiddha, Sarvvavijnanadayini, Kalikalkavihantri, Guhyapanishaduttarma, Nishtha, Drishti.

(68) Smriti, Vyapti, Pushti, Tushti, Kriyavati, Vishvamareshvasreshana, Bhukti, Mukti, Shiva, Amrita.

(69) Lohitasarpamala, Bhishani, Naramalini, Anantashayana, Ananta, Naranarayanodbhava, Nrisimhi, Daityamathini, Shankhachakragadadhara, Ambika.

(70) Sankarshanasamutpatti, Padasamshrava, Mahajvala, Mahabhuti, Sumurti, Sarvvakamadhuka, Suprabha, Sustani, Souri, Dharmakamarthamokshada.

(71) Bhrumadhyanilaya, Purva, Puranapurusharani, Mahavibhutida, Madhya, Sarojanayana, Sama, Anadya, Nilotpaladalaprabha, Asthadashabhuja.

(72) Sarvvashaktyasanaruda, Dharmadharmavivarjita, Vairagyajnananirata, Niraloka, Nirindriya, Vichitragahanadhara, Shvashvatasthanavasini, Sthaneshvari, Nirananda, Trishulavaradharini.

(73) Asheshadevatamurti, Devatavaradevata, Ganambika, Giriputri, Nishumbhavinipatini,

Avarna, Varnarahita, Trivarna, Jivasambhava, Anantavarna.

(74) Ananyastha, Shankari, Shantamanasa, Agotra, Gomati, Goptri, Guhyarupa, Gunottara, Goʻ Gih.

(75) Govyapriya, Gouni, Ganeshvaranamaskrita, Satyabhama, Satyasandha, Trisandhya, Sandhivarjita, Sarvvavadashraya, Samkhya, Samkhyayogasamudbhava.

(76) Asamkhyeya, Aprameyakhya, Shunya, Suddhakulodbhava, Vindunadasamutpatti, Shambhuvasa, Shashiprabha, Pishanga, Bhedarahita, Manojna.

(77) Madhusudani, Mahashri, Shrisamutapatti, Tamohparepratishthita, Tritattvamata, Trividha, Susukshmapadasamshraya, Shantyatita, Malatita, Nirvikara.

(78) Nirashraya, Shivakhya, Chittanilaya, Kashyapı, Shivajnanasvarupini, Daityadana-vanirmukhi, Kalakarnika, Shastrayoni, Kriyamurti, Chatruvargapradarshika.

(79) Narayani, Narodbhuti, Koumudi, Lingadharini, Karmuki, Kalita, Bhava, Paravaravibhutida, Vadava, Pararddhajatamahima.

(80) Vamalochana, Subhadra, Devaki, Sita, Manasvini, Vedavedangaparaga, Manyumata, Mahamanyusamudbhava, Amanyu, Amritasvada.

(81) Puruhuta, Purushtuta, Ashouchya, Bhinnavishaya, Hiranyarajatapriya, Hiranyarajani, Haimi, Hemabharanabhushita, Vibhrajamana, Durjneya.

(82) Jyotishtomafalaprada, Mahanidrasa-mudbhyuti, Anidra, Satyadevata, Dirgha, Kakudmini, Hridya, Shantida, Shantivarddhini, Lakshyadishaktijanani.

(83) Shaktichakrapravartika, Trishaktijanani, Janya, Shadurmiparivarjita, Sudhama, Karmakarani, Yugantadahanatmika, Sankarshini, Jagaddhatri, Kamayoni.

(84) Kiritini, Aindri, Trailokyanamita, Vaishnavi, Parameshvari, Pradyumnadayita, Datri, Yugmadrishti, Trilochana, Madotkata.

(85) Hamsagati, Prachanda, Chandavikrama, Vrishavesha, Vishayanmatra, Vindhyaparvata-vasini, Himavanmerunilaya, Kailasagirivasini, Chanurahantritanaya, Nitijna.

(86) Kamarupini, Vedavedya, Vratasnata, Brahmashailanivasini, Virabhadrapraja, Vira, Siddha, Mahakamasamudbhava, Vidyadharapriya, Vidyadharanirakriti.

(87) Apyayani, Haranti, Pavani, Poshani, Kala, Matrika, Manmathodbhuta, Varija, Vahanapriya, Sudha.

(88) Karishini, Vani, Vinavadanatatpara, Sevita, Sevika, Sevya, Sinivai, Garudatmati, Arundhati, Hiranyakshi.

(89) Mrigakshi, Manadayini, Vasuprada, Vasumati, Vasudhara, Vasundhara, Dharadhara, Vararoha, Characharasahasrada, Shrifala.

(90) Shrimati, Shrisha, Shrinivasa, Shivapriya, Shridhari, Shrikari, Kalya, Shridhararddhasharirini, Anantadrishti, Akshudra.

(91) Dhatrisha, Dhanadapriya, Daityasamuhaniyantri, Simhika, Simhavahana, Suvarchala, Sushroni, Sukirti, Chhinnasamshaya, Rasajna.

(92) Rasada, Rama, Lelihana, Amritasrava, Nityodita, Svayamjyotih, Utsuka, Mritajivani, Vajratunda, Vajrajihva.

(93) Mangalya, Mangala, Mala, Nirmala, Malaharini, Gandharvi, Garudi, Chandri, Kambalashvatarapriya, Soudamini.

(94) Janananda, Bhrikutikutilanana, Karnikarakara, Kakshya, Kamsapranapaharini, Yugandhara, Yugavarta, Trisandhya, Harshavardhini, Pratyakshadevata.

(95) Divya, Divyagandhathivasana, Shakrasanagata, Shakri, Sadhya, Charusharasana, Ishta, Vishishta, Shishteshta, Shishtashishtaprapujita.

(96) Shatarupa, Shatavarta, Vinata, Surabhi, Sura, Surendramata, Sudyumna, Sushumna, Suryasamsthita, Samiksha.

(97) Satpratishtha, Nivritti, Jnanaparaga, Dharmashastrarthakushala, Dharmajna, Dharma-

vahana, Dharmadharmavinirmatri, Dharmika-
mangalaprada, Dharmamayi, Dharmashakti.

(98) Vidharma, Vishvadharmini, Dharmantara,
Dharmamayi, Dharmapurva, Dhanavaha,
Dharmopadeshtri, Dharmaksha, Dharmagamya,
Dharadhara.

(99) Kapalisha, Kalamurti, Kalakalitavigraha,
Sarvvashaktavinirmukta, Sarvvashaktyashraya-
shraya, Sarva, Sarvveshvari, Sukshma, Suksh-
majnanasvarupini, Pradhanapurusheshesha.

(100) Mahadevaikasakshini, Sadashiva, Vishay-
anmurti, Vedamurti, Amurtika, Parameshvari,
Shobha, Vishala, Prasannavadana, Hrishtatma

This completes the list of the one thousand
names given to the goddess. Although Himalaya
had used one thousand and eight names in the
course of his prayers, ten of these names are
missing in the list. You will also have noticed that
a few of the names occur more than once.

## The Line of Uttanapada

I hope you have not forgotten that Svayambhuva
Manu and his wife Shatarupa had a son named
Uttanapada. Uttanapada's brother was Priyavrata.
Dhruva was Uttanapada's son. Dhruva was so
devoted to Vishnu that Vishnu earmarked for him
a place in the heavens known as Dhruvaloka.
(Dhruva became the Pole Star. The complete story
of Dhruva and his *tapasya* is given in the *Vishnu
Purana*.)

Also in Uttanapada's line was born Chaksusha. He became a Manu. (Chakshusha was the sixth Manu of the present *kalpa*). In Chakshusa Manu's line was born Vena, and Vena's son was Prithu. Prithu milked the earth and obtained foodgrains on which people can survive. That is the reason why the earth is known as *prithivi.* (Prithu's story is given in several *Puranas*, in addition to the *Mahabharata* and the *Harivamsha*.)

Prithu's son was Shikhandi and Shikhandi's son was Sushila. Sushila was a very religious person. He faithfully studied the *Vedas* and visited several places of pilgrimage. His travels eventually brought him to the Himalayas, through which the sacred river Mandakini flowed. Near the banks of the river was a beautiful hermitage. It was there that Sushila began to pray to Shiva. While Sushila was thus praying, a sage named Shvetashvatara arrived. The sage's body was lean with *tapasya* and he was smeared with ashes.

Sushila finished praying to Shiva and worshipped the sage. "I am indeed fortunate that I have met you," he told Shvetashvatara. "Please make me your disciple and teach me all that there is to know."

The sage agreed. He taught Sushila and several other disciples the knowledge of the *shastras* (sacred texts).

Shikhandi had a brother named Havirddhana. Havirddhana's son was Prachinavarhi. He married

Savarna, the daughter of the ocean, and had ten
sons. These sons were known as the Prachetas.
The Prachetas were devoted to Vishnu and prayed
to Vishnu for several years. (The *Vishnu Purana*
states that they meditated for ten thousand years
under the ocean.) All ten Prachetas married
Marisha and Daksha was born as a result of this
marriage. (Marisha's story is given in the *Vishnu
Purana.*) It was this Daksha who had earlier been
born as Brahma's son. Because he quarrelled with
Shiva, Shiva cursed Daksha that he would be born
as the son of the Prachetas.

"Tell us the story of Daksha," the sages
requested Lomaharshana.

(The Prachetas are not to be confused with a
sage named Pracheta. The sage Pracheta was
Brahma's son, as per the *Brahmavaivarta Purana.*)

## Daksha's Story

Daksha was Brahma's son and had a daughter
named Sati. Sati was married to Shiva. Daksha
was thus Shiva's father-in-law.

Once Daksha came to visit his son-in-law. But
although Shiva worshipped him with all due
respect, Daksha felt that he had been slighted.
Subsequently, when Sati went to visit her father,
Daksha severely reprimanded her.

"Your husband is worse than useless," he told
his daughter. "My other sons-in-law are far

superior to him. You are not welcome in my house. Return to your worthless husband."

Sati could not bear to hear this abuse of her husband and immolated herself. She was later born as Parvati, the daughter of Himavana (the Himalayas) and married Shiva again.

Shiva was furious to learn that Sati had died. He visited Daksha and cursed him that he would be born on earth as the son of a *kshatriya*. It was thus that Daksha had been born as the son of the Prachetas.

(Daksha's story is full of inconsistencies in the *Puranas*. There is an account of a *yajna* that Daksha performed. Shiva either destroyed this *yajna* himself, or had it destroyed by Virabhadra. But which Daksha performed this *yajna*, the one who was the son of Brahma or the one who was the son of the Prachetas? The *Kurma Purana* suggests that it was the son of the Prachetas who performed this ceremony. The more customary account, such as that in the *Bhagavata Purana*, is that it was Brahma's son who performed the sacrifice. Daksha was angered at Shiva because, on one particular occasion, Shiva did not stand up to show him respect, although Daksha happened to be Shiva's father-in-law. Daksha therefore organised a *yajna* to which he did not invite Shiva. Sati went to the ceremony uninvited, and immolated herself when her father started to criticise her husband. Hearing of Sati's death,

Shiva destroyed the *yajna*. He also cursed Daksha that Daksha would have to be born as the son of the Prachetas.)

To return to the account of the *Kurma Purana*, the Daksha, who was the son of the Prachetas, organised a *yajna*. All the gods and sages were invited to this ceremony. But as a result of Daksha's earlier enmity with his son-in-law, Shiva was not invited.

There was a sage named Dadhichi who protested at this slight to Shiva. "How can you have a religious ceremony without inviting Shiva?" he told Daksha.

"Shiva is a worthless fellow," replied Daksha. "He is not fit to be worshipped together with the other gods. He wears skulls and destroys all that is created. How can he be treated as an equal of the great Vishnu, the preserver of all that one can see? My *yajna* is dedicated to Vishnu. It is not meant for the likes of Shiva."

Dadhichi tried to persuade Daksha that Shiva should not be ignored, but Daksha was in no mood to listen. Dadhichi refused to take part in such a *yajna* and assured Daksha that his ceremony would not be successfully completed. He also cursed the other sages, who had sided with Daksha, that they would go to hell and would deviate from the path laid down in the *Vedas*. (The *Mahabharata* also records Dadhichi's protest. According to the *Mahabharata*, Dadhichi was devoted to Shiva.)

Daksha went ahead with his *yajna*. The other gods, including Vishnu, came to attend the ceremony

Meanwhile, Parvati got to know about the *yajna* and told Shiva, "How can there be a ceremony at which you are not invited? Although Daksha used to be my father in my earlier life, this evil act of his should not be condoned. Please destroy the ceremony."

(If one goes by the more customary account, the question of Parvati's asking Shiva to destroy the *yajna* does not arise. Sati died on the occasion of the ceremony and it was the grief at Sati's death that led Shiva to exact vengeance. This happened much before Parvati was born as the daughter of Himavana.)

Because of Parvati's bidding, Shiva created a demon named Virabhadra. Virabhadra had a thousand heads, a thousand feet, a thousand eyes and a thousand arms. His body shone with radiance like the sun at the time of destruction. The thousand arms held all sorts of weapons in them.

"What are my orders?" Virabhadra asked Shiva.

"Go and destroy Daksha's *yajna*," was the reply.

Virabhadra ascended a bull and set out for Daksha's house. He created thousands and thousands of demons who would aid him in the task of destruction. These demons were armed with spears, tridents, maces, clubs and stones. Parvati also created a goddess named Bhadrakali who would help Virabhadra.

This strange army arrived at the place where the *yajna* was being held and said, "We are Shiva's followers. We have come to receive Shiva's share of the offerings."

"No offerings have been earmarked for Shiva," replied the gods and the sages. "He has not even been invited to the sacrifice."

These words angered Virabhadra and he began his task of destruction. His companions uprooted the scaffoldings that had been erected on the occasion of the sacrifice. The sacrifical horse was flung into the waters of the river Ganga. (This was an *ashwamedha yajna* (horse sacrifice) that was being performed on the banks of the river Ganga.)

Virabhadra caught hold of Bhaga (identified as the sun-god Surya) and tore out his eyes. He smashed the teeth of the god Pusha (also identified as another manifestation of the sun-god Surya). As for the moon-god Chandra, Virabhadra gave him a resounding kick and sent him reeling. The fire-god Agni had his arms and tongue sliced off by Virabhadra's companions. The sages were kicked and boxed.

Vishnu himself came to intervene and Virabhadra began to fight with Vishnu.

Vishnu has a wonderful weapon named *sudarshana chakra* (a bladed-discus) and he hurled this at Virabhadra. But Virabhadra easily repelled this weapon with his arrows. Vishnu is carried by Garuda, king of the birds. Garuda attacked Virabhadra, but so fierce was Virabhadra, that Garuda had to flee. The entire universe marvelled to see that Virabhadra could thus vanquish Vishnu and Garuda.

Brahma now arrived and sought to put an end to the fighting. He started to pray to Shiva and Shiva and Parvati arrived on the scene. The assembled gods and sages also began to pray to Shiva and Parvati. Parvati was moved to pity by these prayers.

"These gods and sages have now sought refuge with you," she told Shiva. "Please pardon them their sins."

"Agreed," replied Shiva. "You have my blessings now. But please remember that one cannot have a religious ceremony without I being worshipped."

The gods and the sages realised that Shiva was no different from Vishnu. They were really one and the same, different manifestations of the same universal force.

When Daksha had earlier been born as the son of Brahma, he had married Asikli, the daughter of Virana. (There is a minor contradiction here as well. Earlier, the *Kurma Purana* has stated that Daksha's wife was Prasuti. It is of course possible that Prasuti and Asikli were different names for the same individual.)

Daksha and Asikli had had one thousand sons. But the sage Narada had persuaded these sons to become hermits, disinterested in worldly pursuits. (The *Vishnu Purana* gives a more complete account. First, five thousand sons named the Haryashvas had been born and Narada had persuaded these sons to become hermits. Next, one thousand sons named the Shavalashvas had been born and these had also become hermits at Narada's instigation. Thereafter, sixty daughters had been born.)

To return to the account of the *Kurma Purana*, Daksha and Asikli had had sixty daughters. Ten of these daughters had been married to Dharma, Brahma's son. (There is again a contradiction. In the section on creation, the *Kurma Purana* had stated that thirteen daughters had been married to Dharma.) The ten daughters who had been married to Dharma were Marutvati, Vasu, Yami, Lamba, Bhanu, Arundhati, Sankalpa, Muhurta, Sadhya and Vishva. Vishva's sons were the gods known as the *vishvadevas*, Sadhya's sons the gods known as the *sadhyas*, Marutvati's sons the gods known as the *maruts*, Vasu's sons the gods known as the *vasus* and Bhanu's sons the gods known as the *bhanus*. (More usually, the *Puranas* have a completely different account of the birth of the *maruts*. They were born as the sons of Diti, Kashyapa's wife.) Muhurta gave birth to time, Lamba to cattle *(ghosha)*, Yami to snakes *(nagas)*,

Arundhati to all the objects *(vishaya)* on earth and Sankalpa to resolution *(sankalpa)*.

Thirteen of Daksha's daughters had been married to the sage Kashyapa. Their names were Aditi, Diti, Arishta, Danu, Surasa, Khasa, Surabhi, Vinata, Tamra, Krodhavasha, Ira, Kadru and Muni. Twelve gods known as the *adityas* were born as the sons of Aditi. Their names were Amsha, Dhata, Bhaga, Tvashta, Mitra, Varuna, Aryama, Vivasvana, Savita, Pusha, Amshumana and Vishnu.

Danu's sons were demons *(danavas)*. Chief among them were Tara, Shambara, Kapila, Shankara, Svarbhanu and Vrishaparva. (Some *Puranas* mention forty such sons.)

Surasa gave birth to the *gandharvas*. (More usually, it is stated that Surasa was the mother of the snakes *(nagas)*.)

Aristha's sons were thousands and thousands of snakes (sarpas).

Kadru's sons were also snakes *(nagas)*.

Tamra's daughters were the ancestors of the birds. Surabhi gave birth to cows and buffaloes and Ira to trees and herbs.

Khasa was the mother of *yakshas* (demi-gods), Muni of *apsaras* and Krodhavasha of *rakshasas*.

Vinata had two sons named Garuda and Aruna. These two sons performed very difficult *tapasya*.

Garuda pleased Vishnu and obtained the boon that he would carry Vishnu around. Aruna pleased Shiva and obtained the boon that he would become the sun's charioteer. (The story of the rivalry between Vinata and Kadru and their respective offspring is given in the *Bhagavata* and *Matsya Puranas*.)

This leaves Diti. She had two sons named Hiranyakashipu and Hiranyaksha. There two sons were demons and their children came to be known as the *daityas*. Hiranyakashipu was elder to Hiranyaksha. (The *Puranas* do not agree on this. In some *Puranas*, Hiranyaksha is referred to as the elder brother.)

## Hiranyakashipu

Hiranyakashipu pleased Brahma through his prayers. As a result of the boon that he received from Brahma, he became invincible and started to oppress the world. He drove the gods out of heaven.

The gods and the sages went to Brahma to persuade him to do something about Hiranyakashipu.

"I cannot really help you," said Brahma. "Go to the northern shores of the great ocean and pray to Vishnu there. I will accompany you. It is Vishnu alone who can find a solution."

Brahma led the gods and the sages to the shores of the great ocean and started to pray to Vishnu there.

Vishnu appeared before them. "Why have all of you come here?" he asked. "What do you want?"

"It is Hiranyakashipu," replied the gods and the sages. "He is oppressing the world thanks to a boon received from Brahma. Because of the boon, he can only be killed by you. Please kill him and save the universe."

Vishnu created a being out of his body. This being was as gigantic as Mount Sumeru and held a lotus (padma), a conch-shell (shankha) and a mace (gada) in his hands. "Go and kill Hiranyakashipu," Vishnu instructed the being.

The being thereupon ascended Garuda and left for Hiranyakashipu's capital. His roars made the ramparts of the city quake.

Hiranyakashipu had four sons named Prahrada, Anuhrada, Samhrada and Hrada. (The more usual names are Prahlada, Anuhlada, Samhlada and Hlada.) Accompanied by Hiranyakashipu's demon soldiers, these four sons came out to fight with the being. They let loose a volley of arrows, but the being easily repelled all of these. The four princes then unleashed divine weapons on the being. Prahrada used brahmastra, Anuhrada vaishnavastra, Samhrada koumarastra and Hrada agneyastra. But these divine weapons could do the wonderful being no harm. He merely picked up the princes and flung them far away.

On seeing that his sons had thus been disposed of, Hiranyakashipu came to fight. He gave the being a resounding kick on his chest and the creature fled in pain to Vishnu.

Vishnu now realised that he would have to take care of Hiranyakashipu himself. He adopted the form of a being who was half-man and half-lion. Since *nara* means man and *simha* means lion, this came to be known as the *narasimha* incarnation (*avatara*) of Vishnu.

"Go and kill this peculiar creature," Hiranyakashipu instructed Prahrada.

Prahrada and his brothers tried to fight with Vishnu, but were defeated essily. Hiranyakashipu now sent his brother Hiranyaksha to fight. Hiranyaksha used several weapons on Vishnu, including the divine weapon known as *pashupata*. But these weapons could do Vishnu no harm.

Meanwhile, Prahrada had realised that this being could be none other than Vishnu. He started to pray to Vishnu. He requested his brothers, uncle and father not to fight with Vishnu. But Hiranyakashipu would not listen. In his form of *narasimha*, Vishnu then tore apart Hiranyakashipu's chest with his claws and thereby killed him. He also killed Anuhrada, Samhrada and Hrada.

(A fairly common story in the *Puranas*, such as the *Vishnu Purana*, is the story of Prahlada. Despite being Hiranyakashipu's son, Prahlada was devoted to Vishnu from his childhood. Hiranyakashipu had no desire to have a son who was devoted to Vishnu and did his level best to kill Prahlada. But Prahlada was protected by Vishnu and survived all these attempts. In the final incident, *narasimha* appeared while Hiranyakashipu was arguing with Prahlada and killed the demon-king. Vishnu then crowned Prahlada king in Hiranyakashipu's place. There was no question of Hiranyaksha becoming king after Hiranyakashipu. In the more common account, Hiranyaksha was the elder brother and had already been killed by Vishnu in his boar *(varaha)* incarnation. It was Hiranyaksha's death that led to Hiranyakashipu's hatred of Vishnu. There is thus some variance between this more common account and that related by the *Kurma Purana*.)

## Hiranyaksha

After Hiranyakashipu died, Hiranyaksha became the king of the demons.

Hiranyaksha promptly began to oppress the world. He defeated the gods and drove them out of heaven. He also took the earth down to the underworld. The gods again went to Brahma in search of a solution and Brahma took them to Vishnu. They prayed to Vishnu so that Hiranyaksha might be killed.

Vishnu adopted the form of a boar and killed Hiranyaksha. He also raised the earth up to its rightful place. (This was the story that we alluded to when the *Kurma Purana* mentioned Vishnu's boar incarnation.)

When Hiranyaksha was killed, Prahrada became the king of the demons. Initially, he ruled well. He worshipped Vishnu and performed *yajnas*. The kingdom thrived and prospered. But on one occasion, Prahrada forgot to worship a *brahmana* through inadvertence.

The *brahmana* was furious as he thought that Prahrada had done this knowingly. "You have dared to ignore me because you think that you are blessed by Vishnu," said the *brahmana*. "I curse you that you will forget all about Vishnu. Your delusions will make you fight with Vishnu and you will lose all your powers."

As a result of the *brahmana's* curse, Prahrada deviated from the righteous path. He ignored the *brahmanas* and the *Vedas*. He desired to have revenge on Vishnu for having killed his father and uncle. Prahrada fought a long and bitter war with Vishnu. When he was eventually defeated by Vishnu, he realised the folly of his evil ways and sought refuge with Vishnu.

After Prahrada's death, Hiranyaksha's son Andhaka became the king of the demons.

## A Digression on Goutama

Many years ago, there was a terrible drought on earth. There was no food to be had and famine prevailed.

There were several sages who lived in the forest, and they too, suffered from a lack of food.

Goutama was a very powerful sage and he had a hermitage in the forest. Such were the powers that Goutama had that it never stopped raining in his hermitage. There was no famine there and plenty of food was to be had. The other sages therefore went to Goutama's hermitage and begged him to provide them with food and shelter. This request Goutama readily agreed to, and the sages lived there happily.

After twelve years had passed, it began to rain again. The drought had passed and foodgrains started to grow. The sages now begged their leave of Goutama.

"Stay for a few more days," said Goutama. "Be my guests and bless my household."

The sages tarried, but they were jealous of Goutama and his powers. They therefore plotted to bring about Goutama's downfall. With their own powers, they created a black calf. This calf was nothing but an illusion. But having created it, the sages sent it to Goutama. Goutama found the calf wandering around and decided to take it to his cowshed. But as soon as he touched the calf, the calf seemed to die. All this was because of the illusion, but Goutama did not know this. He was thunderstruck at having killed a cow.

"You are evil, you have killed a cow," the sages told Goutama. "It would be a sin to remain as your guest. We are leaving."

By then, Goutama had got to know that the calf had been an illusion. He was extremely angry with the sages and cursed them, "Because you have been evil, you will deviate from the path laid down by the *Vedas*. You will rot in hell and will have to be born several times to be freed of your sins."

The sages started to pray to Vishnu and Shiva. They wished that their sins might be cleansed.

"What shall we do with these sages?" Shiva asked Vishnu. "Shall we pardon them? They are praying for deliverance."

"Never," replied Vishnu. "Those who do not follow what is laid down in the *Vedas* will surely rot in hell. But since they are not permitted to follow the sacred *shastras*, let us compose some other *shastras* for them. They will follow those evil *shastras*, rot in hell and be born on earth several times. That is their penance."

To delude the sages, Shiva himself pretended to be a great religious teacher. He preached evil ways and the stupid *brahmanas* began to follow what he preached.

## Andhaka

While Shiva was gone, he left his companion Nandi to look after his household. He also gave

Vishnu the overall responsibility of ensuring that all was well with Parvati and the gods and the sages.

Realising that Shiva was away, Andhaka thought that this was the opportune moment for abducting Parvati. He found that Nandi stood guard at the entrance to Shiva's house and began to fight with Nandi. Nandi struck Andhaka on the chest with a trident.

This angered Andhaka and he created a thousand other demons who were just like him in appearance. This army of demons defeated Nandi and the gods. Nandi did not know what to do and started to pray to Vishnu. Vishnu created some goddesses from his body and these goddesses killed the demon soldiers. Andhaka also fled.

After twelve years had passed, Shiva returned and learnt what had transpired.

By then, Andhaka had recovered and he returned, determined in his bid to abduct Parvati. Both Shiva and Vishnu now started to fight with Andhaka's army.

Vishnu told Shiva, "Kill this demon. No one but you can kill Andhaka. Please kill the demon and deliver the universe."

Shiva pierced Andhaka's chest with a trident. He held the trident aloft, with Andhaka transfixed to one of its prongs. And with his trident held aloft, Shiva began to dance.

But all the evil had deserted Andhaka's body and mind as soon as he had been pierced by Shiva's trident. He started to pray to Shiva. These prayers pleased Shiva.

He lowered the trident and told Andhaka, "I am pleased with your prayers. My companions are known as the *ganas*. Stay by my side and be a *ganapati*, that is, a lord over the *ganas*. You will be Nandi's companion."

**Vali**

With Andhaka thus taken care of, Prahrada's son Virochana became the king of the demons. He ruled his kingdom well.

There was a sage named Sanatakumara who once went to visit Virochana. Virochana was delighted to see the sage and Sanatakumara instructed Virochana on the true nature of the universe. These teachings so impressed Virochana that he no longer had any desire to be a king. He went off to meditate, after having crowned his son, Vali, as the king of the demons.

Vali was a good and righteous king. He ruled well and observed religious rites faithfully. But he defeated Indra and the other gods and won over heaven from them. Indra and the other gods started to pray to Vishnu for deliverance.

The mother of all the gods was Aditi and she was despondent at seeing her children suffer thus. She too, started to pray to Vishnu. Stirred by these prayers, Vishnu appeared before Aditi.

"What boon do you desire?" he asked.

"Please grant me the boon that you will be born as my son," replied Aditi. "And as my son, you will take care of Vali."

Vishnu granted the boon and was born as Aditi's son. As Aditi's son, Vishnu studied the *Vedas* under the sage Bharadvaja.

Meanwhile, Vali arranged a *yajna* and Vishnu came to attend the ceremony in the form of a dwarf *(vamana)*. (In more usual accounts, such as the *Bhagavata Purana*, Vishnu was born as a dwarf.)

Vali was not going to refuse anything to anyone on the occasion of the sacrifice. As soon as he saw the dwarf, he worshipped him and said, "I am fortunate that you have come to attend my ceremony. Please tell me what I can do for you."

"Grant me as much of land as can be covered in three of my footsteps," replied the dwarf.

This boon Vali granted. The dwarf immediately assumed a gigantic form. With one footstep, Vishnu covered the entire earth. With a second, he covered the sky. And with the third and final footstep, he covered heaven. The entire universe is inside an egg *(anda)* and outside the egg there is water. Vishnu's foot cracked the shell of the egg and some of the water that was outside, poured in. This water began to flow through the sky and became the heavenly Ganga. (The story of the heavenly Ganga (identified as the Milky Way) descending to earth is a separate story. The story of Ganga being born from Vishnu's body is given in the *Brahmavaivarta Purana*.)

Having traversed all the land that was available, Vishnu resumed his form of a dwarf.

"You have now donated to me all the three worlds," he told Vali. "Where will you stay?"

"I seek refuge with you," was Vali's answer.

Vishnu then instructed Vali to go and live in the underworld. As for heaven, it was restored to Indra.

This is the story of Vishnu's dwarf *(vamana)* incarnation.

## Vana

Vali had a hundred sons, the eldest among whom was Vana. Vana was devoted to Shiva. He was also extremely powerful. He defeated Indra and conquered the three worlds.

Indra and the other gods went to Shiva. "Your devotee, Vana, is oppressing us," they told Shiva. "Please take care of him."

Shiva took up a single arrow and with this, he completely burnt up Vana's city.

(This is deviation from the usual account of the *Puranas*, such as the *Vishnu Purana* or the

*Bhagavata Purana.* In those accounts, Krishna fought with Vana and defeated him, although Shiva fought on Vana's side. It was because of Krishna's blessings that Vana became Shiva's companion. Vana's capital was named Shonitapura.)

When Vana's city was being burnt up, Vana emerged and started to pray to Shiva's *linga* (image of Shiva). Pleased at Vana's prayers, Shiva made Vana a *ganapati.* Thus, Vana came to be Shiva's constant companion.

## The Solar Dynasty

The sun-god, Vivasvana, was the son of Kashyapa and Aditi. He had four wives, Samjna, Rajni, Prabha and Chhaya.

Samjna's son was Vaivasvata Manu. Rajni's children were Yama, Yamuna and Revanta. Savarni, Shani, Tapati and Vishti were Chhaya's children and Prabha's son was Prabhata.

(The names do not tally across the *Puranas.* For example, in the *Markandeya Purana,* the sun had only two wives, Samjna and Chhaya. Yama and Yamuna were also the children of Samjna.)

Vaivasvata Manu had nine sons. Their names were Ikshvaku, Nabhaga, Dhrishta, Sharyati, Narishyanta, Nabhaga, Arishta, Karusha and Prishadhra. Manu also had a daughter named Ila, from whom the lunar dynasty originated.

Ikshvaku's son was Vikukshi and this was the line of Kakutstha. In this line was born Rama, of *Ramayana* fame.

The names of several kings of the solar dynasty are given. But these we will not reproduce, as they are merely a catalogue of names.

## The Lunar Dynasty

Budha was the son of the moon-god Chandra. Budha married Ila and they had a son named Pururava.

Pururava married the *apsara* Urvashi and they had six sons. One of these sons was Ayu and amongst Ayu's descendants was a king named Yayati.

Yayati had two wives. The first was Devayani, daughter of Shukracharya, the preceptor of the demons. The second wife was named Sharmishtha and she was the daughter of Vrishaparva, the king of the *danavas*. Yayati and Devayani had two sons, Yadu and Turvasu. Yayati and Sharmishtha had three sons, Druhya, Anu and Puru. When it became time for Yayati to retire to the forest, he gave Puru the bulk of the kingdom and Puru's descendants came to be known as the Pauravas. Yadu was given some land towards the south-west and his descendants were the Yadavas. Turvasu ruled to the south-east, Druhya to the west and Anu to the north.

One of Yadu's descendants was the king Kritavirya and Kritavirya's son became famous as Kartavirya Arjuna. He had a thousand arms and was the most skilled of fighters. He eventually met his death at the hands of Parashurama.

Kartavirya Arjuna had several hundred sons. But the five most important ones were Shura, Shurasena, Krishna, Dhrishna and Jayadvaja. Jayadvaja was devoted to Vishnu, but his brothers were more inclined towards the worship of Shiva.

The four brothers told Jayadhvaja, "Stop worshipping Vishnu. Our father was a devotee of Shiva's and it is our duty to follow the example set by our father. Let us worship Shiva."

"It is my duty to worship Vishnu," replied Jayadhvaja. "Vishnu is the lord of everything, he is the preserver. How can I do otherwise.?"

The brothers debated about the virtues of worshipping Shiva vis-a-vis Vishnu, but could arrive at no consensus. They therefore decided to seek the advice of the seven great sages (saptarshi), chief amongst whom was Vashishtha.

Vashishtha told the brothers, "One worships the god that one chooses, there are no rules in this regard. All gods yield the desired fruit, if properly worshipped. To the extent that there are rules, these are as follows. Kings worship Vishnu and Indra; brahmanas worship Agni, Aditya, Brahma and Shiva; the gods worship Vishnu; the demons worship Shiva; the yakshas and gandharvas worship Chandra; the sages worship Brahma and Shiva; and women worship Parvati. But for humans, the best way is to realise that Shiva is no different from Vishnu and that Shiva and Vishnu should therefore be worshipped simultaneously."

The *Kurma Purana* also gives the names of several kings belonging to the lunar dynasty. But these we will gloss over, as they are merely only a catalogue of names.

## Durjaya and Urvashi

There used to be a king named Durjaya. He was learned in the *shastras* and a good king. His wife was a beautiful and good woman.

One day, King Durjaya went to the banks of the river Kalindi. There he met the *apsara* Urvashi and fell in love with her. He married Urvashi and lived with her for many years.

After several years had passed, Durjaya remembered his kingdom and wife. He told Urvashi, "Please let me return to my home now."

"Not yet, king," replied Urvashi. "Please stay with me for one more year."

"I will return as soon as I have visited my kingdom," said Durjaya. "I promise you that I will not tarry there. Therefore, let me return."

"I will let you go on condition that you do not live as the husband of any other woman," replied Urvashi.

Durjaya agreed to this condition and returned home. But because of the word that he had given Urvashi, he stayed away from his wife and did not venture near her. His wife tried to find out what the matter was, but Durjaya would not reply. Finally, the queen got to know what Durjaya had done and realised that her husband had committed a sin. He should not have married Urvashi while his wife was still alive. The queen therefore told Durjaya, "You have sinned. You must perform penance. That is the sort of action that befits a king, not this despondency that you have become addicted to."

King Durjaya went and met the sage Kanva to ascertain what sort of penance should be performed for the sin that he had committed. Kanva advised him to go to the Himalayas and meditate.

While Durjaya was going to the Himalayas, he met a *gandharva* king. The *gandharva* king wore a divine garland around his neck. As soon as he saw the garland, Durjaya remembered Urvashi. He thought that the garland was a fitting adornment for no one but Urvashi. He began to fight with the *gandharva* over the possession of the garland. Durjaya managed to defeat the *gandharva* king and obtain the garland. He immediately hastened to the banks of the river Kalindi, because he thought that he might find Urvashi there. But Urvashi was not to be found, and Durjaya roamed the world in search of her.

Finally, Durjaya arrived in the region of Mount Sumeru. The lake Manasa is located there. And by the shores of the lake, Durjaya found Urvashi. He gave the *apsara* the garland and lived happily with her for some time.

After a few days had passed, Urvashi asked Durjaya, "King, please tell me what transpired when you went home."

Durjaya thereupon told Urvashi about the conversation that he had had with his wife and about what the sage Kanva had asked him to do.

Urvashi was alarmed when she heard the king's account. "What have you done?" she exclaimed. "Hasten back, otherwise Kanva and your wife will curse the two of us."

But Durjaya was so smitten with love for Urvashi that he refused to listen to Urvashi's entreaties. Urvashi therefore made herself very ugly. This repelled Durjaya, and he gave Urvashi up.

For twelve years Durjaya performed difficult *tapasya*, living only on fruits and roots. For another twelve years, he lived only on air. After having thus meditated for twenty-four years, Durjaya went to Kanva's hermitage and told the sage all that he had done.

"I am pleased that you have realised the folly of your ways and have performed *tapasya*," said Kanva. "But that alone is not enough. Your sin has been too severe. Go to the city of Varanasi and live there. Shiva is ever-present in that city and he will pardon all your sins."

Durjaya did this and was pardoned all his sins. Such are the benefits of praying to Shiva and such are the virtues of the wonderful city of Varanasi.

## Krishna's Tapasya

Krishna was the eighth incarnation of Vishnu and he was born as the son of Devaki and Vasudeva.

Initially, Krishna did not have any sons Desirous of obtaining a son, Krishna went to visit the sage Upamanyu. The sage's hermitage was beautiful. Wonderous were the trees and flowers that grew there. The constant chanting of the *Vedas* could be heard. Wild animals lost their ferocity as soon as they entered the hemitage. Lotus flowers bloomed in the ponds. Sages came from all over the country to meditate in the hermitage. The sacred river Ganga flowed past the hermitage.

Krishna greeted the sages and they worshipped him in return.

Upamanyu welcomed Krishna with various offerings and said, "Our meditation has been amply rewarded by your visit. The great Vishnu has himself come to grace us by your presence. But is there any particular reason as to why you have come to the hermitage?"

"I wish to meet Shiva," replied Krishna. "How does one get to meet him?"

"Shiva appears if a devotee performs difficult *tapasya*," said Upamanyu. "It helps if the meditation is accompanied by great faith."

Hearing these words, Krishna began a difficult religious rite known as *pashupata vrata*. He donned clothes made out of the barks of trees, smeared ashes on his body and continuously chanted Shiva's name. After many years had passed, Shiva and Parvati appeared before Krishna.

"Krishna, why are you performing *tapasya*?" asked Shiva. "You are the great Vishnu himself. Any object that you desire is immediately attained. Why are you then engaged in this task of meditation?"

"I wish to have a son who is just like you," said Krishna. "Please let him also be devoted to you."

Shiva gladly granted the boon and the son who was born was Shamba (alternatively, Samba). He was the son of Krishna and Jambavati.

(Stories about Shamba are to be found in the *Vishnu Purana*, and also in the *Mahabharata*.)

## The Eras

You probably remember that there are four *yugas* or eras - *satya yuga* or *krita yuga*, *treta yuga*, *dvapara yuga* and *kali yuga*.

Lomaharshana next told the sages about the characteristics of these four eras.

*Kali yuga* is the worst of the four eras. People are sinful and forget the *dharma* of the four *varnas* and the four *ashramas*. In fact, men are so sinful that no prescribed penance atones for their sins. The only place which is free from such sins is the sacred city of Varanasi.

In *satya yuga*, the best course to be pursued is meditation; in *treta yuga* it is the pursuit of knowledge *(jnana)*; in *dvapara yuga* it is the performance of *yajnas*; and in *kali yuga* it is the donation of alms. Brahma is the primary god in *satya yuga*, Surya in *treta yuga*, Vishnu in *dvapara yuga* and Shiva in *kali yuga*.

Envy and jealousy were unknown in *satya yuga* and everyone was happy. There were no superiors and inferiors and all individuals were equally healthy and equally handsome. There were no fixed places for people to live in, no cities and no villages. Men lived in the mountains and on the shores of the oceans.

In *satya yuga*, water was always freely available. This was no longer the case in *treta yuga*. Water only became available when it rained. Rain was unknown earlier. And as it rained, trees began to grow. People lived on these trees. The fruit from these trees provided the sustenance required to make a living. But gradually, anger and jealousy came to be known and many of the wonderful trees disappeared as mankind picked up evil ways. However, enough trees were left to ensure that people did not die of starvation. They lived on honey gathered from the trees. Although men looked on *satya yuga* with nostalgia, ill-health and disease continued to be unknown even in *treta yuga*. But towards the end of *treta yuga*, people became really sinful. All the trees disappeared. To make a living, mankind had to resort to agriculture and animal husbandry. The weather became inclement and seasons like summer, monsoon and winter led to hardship. Notions of property were also introduced. Individuals appropriated mountains, rivers, land, trees and herbs as their own. To instil righteousness in the minds of people, the principles of *varnashrama dharma* were set out towards the end of *treta yuga*.

In *dvapara yuga*, hatred, anger and jealousy became much more common. Fighting started. It was then that Vedavyasa spread amongst ordinary people, the knowledge that was in the *Vedas*, by dividing them. Drought, death and disease came to be known in *dvapara yuga*.

In *kali yuga*, fraudulence is the norm. There are severe droughts and famines, revolutions take place. People are liars and sinners. They are easily angered. They do not respect the *brahmanas*. The *brahmanas*, on their part, forget all about the *Vedas* and *yajnas*. *Shudras* become kings and oppress the *brahmanas*. Some *shudras* shave off their heads and wear saffron clothes. They pretend to be religious teachers. And horror of horrors, people start to believe in these fraudulent teachers. Women wear hairpins in their hair. As if this alone were not enough, they refuse to obey their husbands. Thieves are everywhere. The only redeeming feature of *kali yuga* is the fact that even if one worships Shiva just a little bit in *kali yuga*, one attains undying *punya* (store of merit).

## Lingas

A *linga* is an image of Shiva. There are several wonderful *lingas* in the wonderful city of Varanasi.

There is a gigantic *linga* named Omkara. Amongst other famous *lingas* located in the city are Krittivaseshvara, Madhyadeshvara, Vishveshvara and Kaparddishvara.

The *Kurma Purana* recites the glories of these *lingas*. It also enumerates the various *tirthas* (places of pilgrimage) that are to be found in the city of Varanasi

It goes on to list the virtues of the Ganga, the Yamuna and the city of Prayaga (modern Allahabad).

## Geography and Astronomy

I hope you have not forgotten that Svayambhuva Manu had a son named Priyavrata. Priyavrata had ten sons. Their names were Agnidhra, Agnivahu, Vapushmana, Dyutimana, Medha, Medhatithi, Bhavya, Savana, Putra and Jyotishmana.

Medha, Agnivahu and Putra had no desire to rule. They were not interested in material pursuits and became hermits.

Priyavrata divided the earth amongst the remaining seven sons. Thus it was that the earth came to be divided into seven regions or *dvipas*. The names of these regions are Jambudvipa, Plakshadvipa, Shalmalidvipa, Kushadvipa, Krounchadvipa, Shakadvipa and Pushkaradvipa. Agnidhra ruled over Jambudvipa, Medhatithi over Plakshadvipa, Vapushmana over Shalmalidvipa, Jyotishmana over Kushadvipa, Dyutimana over Krounchadvipa, Bhavya over Shakadvipa and Savana over Pushkaradvipa.

Agnidhra, the ruler of Jambudvipa, had nine sons. Their names were Nabhi Kimpurusha, Hari, Ilavrita, Ramya, Hiranyavana, Kuru, Bhadrashva and Ketumala. Agnidhra divided Jambudvipa into nine regions (*varshas*) and gave each of his sons a region to rule over. A king named Bharata was one of Nabhi's descendants. After the name of Bharata, the region that Nabhi ruled over has come to be known as Bharatavarsha.

There are fourteen regions (*lokas*) in the universe. Seven of them form the upper regions. Their names are *bhuloka, bhuvarloka, svarloka, maharloka, janaloka, tapoloka* and *satyaloka*. *Bhuloka* is the earth and its limits extend upto the points that can be lit up by the rays of the sun and the moon. Take the distance from *bhuloka* to the solar circle. An equal distance beyond the solar circle constitutes *bhuvarloka*. The region from the limits of *bhuvarloka* to the region of Dhruva (the Pole Star) is *svarloka* or *svarga* (heaven). Above the solar circle is the lunar circle and above that come, successively, the regions of the stars *(nakshatras)*, Budha (Mercury), Shukra (Venus), Mangala (Mars), Brihaspati (Jupiter), the *saptarshis'* (the constellation Ursa Majoris or the Great Bear) and Dhruva.

Shani (Saturn), Brihaspati and Mangala move slowly. The sun, the moon, Budha and Shukra move relatively fast. The sun's chariot is drawn by seven horses named Gayatri, Vrihati, Ushnika, Jagati, Pamkti, Anushtupa and Trishtupa. In each month, the sun adopts a specific form known as an *aditya*. There are thus twelve *adityas* - Dhata, Aryama, Mitra, Varuna, Shakru, Vivasvana, Pusha, Parjanya, Amshu, Bhaga, Tvashta and Vishnu.

*Maharloka* is above the world of Dhruva *(dhruvaloka)*. It is reserved for those who have been freed from the bonds of the world. *Janaloka* is still further away. Brahma's sons live there. *Tapoloka* is beyond *janaloka* and *satyaloka* is beyond *tapoloka*. Another word for *satyaloka* is *brahmaloka*, since Brahma lives there. Vishnu lives there as well.

(The *Kurma Purana* does not mention the seven *lokas* that constitute the lower regions of the universe. This is the underworld *(patala)*.)

There are seven seas that surround the seven *dvipas* on earth. The names of the seas are Kshara,

Ikshu, Sura, Ghrita, Dadhi, Kshira and Svadu. (The names of the seven oceans often differ from *Purana* to *Purana*.)

Right in the centre of Jambudvipa is Mount Sumeru. To its south lie the mountains Himavana, Hemakuta and Nishadha; and to its north the mountains Nila, Shveta and Shringi. Bharatavarsha is to the south of Mount Sumeru. Brahma's assembly is located on the peak of Mount Sumeru.

## Manvantaras

You already know what a *manvantara* is. The titles of the seven great sages (*saptarshi*), the names of the gods and the title of Indra change from one *manvantara* to another.

In the present *kalpa* (cycle), six *manvantaras* have passed.

The first Manu was Svayambhuva.

The second Manu was Svarochisha. The gods then were the *paravatas* and *tushitas* and the title of Indra was held by Vipashchita. The seven great sages were Urjja, Stamba, Prana, Dambholi, Vrishabha, Timira and Arvarivana.

Uttama was the third Manu. The gods of this *manvantara* were the *sudhamas*, *satyas*, *shivas*, *pratardanas* and *vashavartis* and the name of the Indra was Sushanti. Rajah, Gotra, Urddhavahu, Savana, Anagha, Sutapa and Shukra were the seven great sages.

The fourth Manu was Tamasa. The gods of this era were the *suravas*, *haris*, *satyas* and *sudhas* and the title of Indra was held by Shibi. The seven great sages were Jyotirdhama, Prithu, Kavya, Chaitra, Agni, Varuna and Pivara.

In the fifth *manvantara*, the Manu was Raivata and the title of Indra was held by Vibhu. The gods were the *bhutis* and the *vaikunthas* and the seven great sages were Hiranyaroma, Vedashri, Urddhavahu, Vedavahu, Suvahu and Suparjanya. (The name of the seventh great sage is missing.)

The Manus Svarochisha, Uttama, Tamasa and Raivata were all descended from Svayambhuva Manu.

The sixth Manu was Chakshusha and the Indra then was Manojava. The gods were known as the *adyas*, *prasutas*, *bhavyas*, *prithukas* and *lekhas*. Sumedha, Viraja, Havishmana, Uttama, Madhu, Abhimana and Sahishnu were the seven great sages.

The seventh *manvantara* is the one that is now current and the Indra now is Purandara. The Manu is Shraddhadeva, the gods are the *adityas*, the *vasus*, the *rudras* and the *maruts*. The names of the seven great sages are Vashishtha, Kashyapa, Atri, Jamadagni, Goutama, Vishvamitra and Bharadvaja.

In the present *kalpa*, there will be seven more *manvantaras* in the future. Thereafter, the world wil be destroyed.

(It should be mentioned that the names given in this section do not necessarily tally with the names given in the other *Puranas*. Not only do the names of the gods, the sages and the Indras differ, the names of the future *manvantaras* also sometimes differ from *Purana* to *Purana*.)

## Vedavyasa

In every *dvapara yuga*, a Vedavyasa is born so as to divide the *Vedas* and disseminate their knowledge. In the present era, there have been twenty-eight *dvapara yugas* and there have therefore been twenty-eight individuals who have held the title of Vedavyasa. The *Kurma Purana* gives their names as follows.

(1) Svayambhuva Manu.

(2) Prajapati.

(3) Ushana.

(4) Brihaspati.

(5) Savita.

(6) Mrityu.

(7) Indra.

(8) Vashishtha.

(9) Sarasvata.

(10) Tridhama.

(11) Rishabha.

(12) Suteja.

(13) Dharma.

(14) Sachakshu.

(15) Trayaruni.

(16) Dhananjaya.

(17) Kritanjaya.

(18) Ritanjaya.

(19) Bharadvaja.

(20) Goutama.

(21) Vachashrava.

(22) Narayana.

(23) Trinavindu.

(24) Valmiki.

(25) Shaktri.

(26) Parashara.

(27) Jatukarna.

(28) Krishna Dvaipayana. Krishna Dvaipayana Vedavyasa divided the *Vedas* into four parts and taught them to four of his disciples. He taught Paila the *Rig Veda*, Vaishampayana the *Yajur Veda*, Jaimini the *Sama Veda* and Sumantu the *Atharva Veda*. As for the *Puranas*, they were taught to Lomaharshana.

## Shiva's Incarnations

Most *Puranas* only mention Vishnu's incarnations *(avataras)*. The *Kurma Purana* is one of the rare ones which mentions Shiva's incarnations.

In each *kali yuga*, Shiva has had an incarnation The names of these incarnations are as follows.

(1) Shveta.

(2) Sutara.

(3) Madana.

(4) Suhotra.

(5) Kankana.

(6) Lokakshi.

(7) Jaigishavya.

(8) Dadhivaha.

(9) Rishabha.

(10) Bhrigu

(11) Ugra.

(12) Atri.

(13) Vali.

(14) Goutama.

(15) Vedashirsha.

(16) Gokarna.

(17) Shikhandaka.

(18) Jatamali.

(19) Attahasa.

(20) Daruka.

(21) Langali.

(22) Mahayama.

(23) Muni.

(24) Shuli.

(25) Pindamunishvara.

(26) Sahishnu.

(27) Somasharma.

(28) Nakulishvara.

## The Ishvara Gita

While Lomaharshana was reciting the *Kurma Purana* to the assembled sages, Krishna Dvaipayana Vedavyasa arrived on the scene. Lomaharshana and the other sages requested Vedavyasa to instruct them about the path to true knowledge. This is what Vedavyasa told them.

The *paramatman* (the divine soul) is the only truth. It is ever pure and ever present. It is from the *paramatman* that the universe is created and it is into the *paramatman* that the universe merges at the time of its destruction. The *paramatman* is not the earth. It is not water, energy, wind or sky. It cannot be touched, nor can it be sensed.

The *paramatman* is always present in the *jivatman* (human soul). Any sense of distinction between the *paramatman* and the *jivatman* is due to illusions and the presence of the ego. The truly learned rise above such illusions. Therefore, a wise person does not see any distinction between his own self and other objects. The same *paramatman* pervades everything. Just as all rivers unite with the ocean, a learned person realises that all individual *jivatmans* unite with the *paramatman*.

*Yoga* (literally, union) is a technique of meditation that helps to bring about this sense of identity between the *jivatman* and the *paramatman*. *Yoga* has eight components. The first is *pranayama*. This means the control of one's breath. The breath of life is known as *prana* and *ayama* means control. There are three parts to any *pranayama* exercise. When the breath is being exhaled, that is known as *rechaka;* and the process of inhalation is known as *puraka*. When the breath is neither being inhaled nor exhaled, that is *kumbhaka*.

The second component of *yoga* is *pratyahara*. This connotes the control of one's senses. *Yoga* must always be performed in a proper posture and this is the third component of *asana*. The fourth component is called *yama*. This means the practice of non-violence, truthfulness and pity. The fifth component is known as *niyama*. This encompasses worship, studying the *Vedas*, cleanliness and meditation.

*Yoga* has a sixth component named *dhyana*. In this process, one conjures up an image of the *paramatman* and meditates continuously on it. The process of fixing this image in one's heart is the seventh component, *dharana*. And the final component, *samadhi*, is a situation where the individual realises the complete identity between the *jivatman* and the *paramatman*.

## Rituals

The sacred thread *(upavita)* ceremony is very important and must always be performed at eight years of age. Brahma had created the cotton tree so that sacred threads might be made out of cotton. But on occasions it is permissible to make sacred threads out of grass.

A *guru* (teacher) is always to be respected and worshipped. In principle, a *guru* is anyone from whom knowledge might be gained. But apart from usual teachers, a father, an elder brother, a king, an uncle, a father-in-law, a grandfather and an individual belonging to a superior *varna* are also recognised as *gurus*. A mother, a grandmother, a *guru's* wife, an aunt, a mother-in-law and the wife of an elder brother are recognised as being equivalent to a *guru*. One must never sit on the same seat as one's *guru*. Nor must a *guru* ever be shown disrespect or argued with. A person who hates his *guru* is certain to go to hell

Amongst *gurus* or those who are equivalent to *gurus*, the most important are a father, a mother, a teacher, an elder brother and a husband. These have to be respectfully served at all costs.

A *brahmana* must always wash his mouth after eating, drinking, sleeping, bathing, spitting or changing clothes. The mouth must also be washed before sitting down to study. It is also recommended that the mouth be washed after talking to those who do not believe in the *Vedas*, *shudras*, outcasts and women. If a mouthwash is not possible, one can cleanse oneself by touching a fire, a cow or the water of the Ganga. If a dirty piece of clothing is touched inadvertently, the act of purification requires the touching of water, wet grass or the earth.

One of the most sacred *mantras* (incantations) that one can chant is the *gayatri.* Before chanting, thirty-two cells must be drawn, as shown, and the letters of the *mantra* must be written down in the cells, as indicated. To recite the *gayatri,* one now reads the letters as they occur in the numbered cells. That is, one starts with cell number one, moves to cell number two and so on and so forth.

| 5 vvr | 13 sya | 21 pra | 29 se | 28 ja | 20 nah | 12 va | 4 tu |
|---|---|---|---|---|---|---|---|
| 6 re | 14 dhi | 22 cho | 30 sa | 27 ra | 19 yo | 11 de | 3 vi |
| 7 ni | 15 ma | 23 da | 31 va | 26 ro | 18 yo | 10 rgo | 2 tsa |
| 8 yam | 16 hi | 24 yat | 32 dom | 25 pa | 17 dhi | 9 bha | 1 ta |

The *Vedas* must never be read at the time of an eclipse. Nor must they be read when a funeral ceremony is going on. It is forbidden to read the *Vedas* while lying on one's bed, or after eating meat. Other periods which are taboo are times when storms are raging or on nights of the new moon. These are some specified trees under which the *Vedas* must never be read.

A person who kills a *brahmana*, drinks wine, or steals gold from a *brahmana*, has to perform penance by killing himself. A person who kills a *brahmana* may also build a hut in the forest and live there for a period of twelve years. But throughout the period, he has to bear a mark signifying the dead *brahmana's* head on his palm. He is also not permitted to visit another *brahmana* or a temple as long as the penance is going on. It needs to be mentioned that the sin of killing a *brahmana* can be thus pardoned only if the killing was done inadvertently. If the killing was conscious, no penance will suffice. Under such circumstances, the sinner had best immolate himself in a fire, drown himself, or fast to death.

For other sins, the observance of a religious rite *(vrata)* is often indicated. The major *vratas* are as follows.

(i) *Santapana*: This involves living for one whole day on cow's urine, cowdung, cow's milk, curds made from cow's milk and clarified butter made from cow's milk. The next day is a day of fasting.

(ii) *Mahasantapana*: This is a more severe verison of the earlier *vrata*. In the case of *santapana vrata*, five items were listed as permissible food. *Mahasantapana vrata* lasts for a period of six days, and on each of these days, only one of the five items mentioned may be partaken of. The seventh day is a day of fasting.

(iii) *Prajapatya* or *krichha*: If this *vrata* is to be observed, one can eat only during the day. For the first three days, one is only permitted to eat twenty-six handfuls of food, each handful being as large as a hen's egg.

For the next three days, twenty-two handfuls are permitted, but only in the evenings. And for the final three days, twenty-four handfuls are permitted.

(iv) *Atikrichha*: This is a more severe version of the earlier *vrata*. For the first three days, a single handful of food is permitted during the day. For the next three days, one handful is permitted in the evenings. One handful can be eaten at any time during the day for the ensuing three days. The final three days are days of fasting. The *vrata* thus lasts for a period of twelve days.

(v) *Paraka*: Twelve continuous days of fasting are required for this.

(vi) *Taptakrichha*: This *vrata* lasts for a period of twelve days, during which time one is permitted to bathe only once a day. For the first three days one drinks only water; for the next three days one lives on milk; one has to live on clarified butter for the ensuing three days; and the final three days are days of fasting.

(vii) *Krichhatikrichha*: If one is to observe this *vrata*, one has to live only on milk for the space of twenty-one days.

(viii) *Padakrichha*: This *vrata* lasts for four days. For the first day one eats only one meal; the second day is a day of fasting; on the third day one can eat as much as one wants; and on the fourth and final day, one fasts.

(ix) *Chandrayana*: This *vrata* lasts for an entire month and begins on the day of the full moon *(purnima)*. On the first day, fifteen handfuls are to be eaten. Thereafter, one handful less is eaten on successive days, until, on the day of the new moon *(amavasya)*, one fasts completely. On each day that follows, the amount of food eaten is increased by one handful. Finally, on the day of the next full moon, fifteen handfuls of food are eaten and the *vrata* is completed.

As mentioned earlier, those who kill *brahmanas*, steal their gold, or drink wine, are sinners. Also sinners are those who associate with these afore-mentioned sinners for more than one year. Those who assoicate with outcasts for more than a year are also sinners.

A *brahmana* who drinks wine should drink boiling wine as a penance. It is also permitted to drink cow's urine as atonement. A person who steals gold from *brahmanas* will go to the king and confess his guilt. His penance will be completed when the king beats him to death with a club. The only exception is a case where the thief himself happens to be a *brahmana*. He can then perform penance by meditating. It is always a king's duty to punish sinners. If the king fails in this task, the sins vest with the king.

A person who associates with sinners has to observe *taptakrichha vrata* for one year. A man who takes an outcast for a wife has to observe *taptakrichha* or *santapana*. A *brahmana* who kills a *kshatriya* is required to observe *prajapatya*, *santapana* or *taptakrichha* for one year. In case the victim is a *vaishya*, *krichhatikrichha* or *chandrayana* are indicated. If a *shudra* is killed, five hundred cows have to be donated. If an elephant is killed, *taptakrichha vrata* has to be observed. *Chandrayana* will suffice if a cow is killed inadvertently. But if a cow is consciously killed, there is no penance that is adequate.

For minor thefts, the stolen goods have to be returned to the rightful owner and *santapana* observed. But if a *brahmana* steals foodgrains, he has to observe *prajapatya* for an entire year. A cannibal can purify himself through *chandrayana vrata*. A person who eats the meat of a crow, dog or elephant, has to observe *taptakrichha*. *Santapana* is for those who happen to eat mongooses, owls or cats. An eater of camels or donkeys observes *taptakrichha*.

A *brahmana* who becomes an atheist can cleanse himself through *prajapatya*. If he revolts against the gods or against his *guru*, the act of purification involves *taptakrichha*. A *brahmana* who recites the *Puranas* to outcasts has to observe *chandrayana*.

There are several other forms of penance that are catalogued by the *Kurma Purana*.

## The Sita who was an Illusion

I am certain that you know the story of the *Ramayana* and you therefore also known that Ravana, the king of Lanka, abducted Sita, Rama's wife. But I am also certain that you do not know the story of the Sita who was an illusion *(maya sita)*.

This story clearly illustrates that no harm can come to a person who is righteous.

Ravana disguised himself as a hermit and came to abduct Sita. But Sita got to know of Ravana's plan and was determined to foil it. She therefore began to pray to Agni, the god of fire

Thus stirred by Sita's prayers, Agni appeared and produced a Sita who was really an illusion. This *maya sita* he left in the real Sita's place. As for the real Sita, she was absorbed into the fire. Without realising the substitutions, Ravana abducted the illusory Sita and the entire war was fought over a Sita who was not even real.

When Rama triumphed over Ravana and recovered Sita, a test by fire *(agni pariksha)* was held.

In the process, the Sita who was an illusion was returned to the fire and the real Sita emerged once again. Thus the real Sita was never tainted by Ravana's touch.

(The story of the Sita who was an illusion is also given in the *Brahmavaivarta Purana.*)

## Shiva and Brahma

Many years ago, Brahma lost his head slightly. He began to imagine that he was superior to Shiva and Vishnu. He told all the sages, "I am the supreme godhead. There is no one else but me."

While Brahma was thus instructing the sages, Vishnu arrived and was enraged at Brahma's behaviour. "You are indeed ignorant," he told Brahma. "I am the supreme godhead. You are only the creator. But I am, after all, the preserver."

While Vishnu and Brahma were thus arguing, the four *Vedas* adopted animate forms and appeared before them. Each of the *Vedas* tried to persuade Brahma and Vishnu that Shiva was superior to both of them. Vishnu was persuaded by this reasoning, but Brahma was not.

He told the *Vedas*, "You must be joking. How can Shiva be superior to the two of us? He is always wandering around with ghosts and demons for companions."

While all this was going on, who should arrive but Shiva? Brahma promptly proceeded to insult Shiva. Shiva then created a being named Kalabhairava from his own body and Kalabhairava started to fight with Brahma. In those days, Brahma used to have five heads. In course of the fighting, Kalabhairava chopped off one of Brahma's heads. Ever since that day, Brahma has had four heads and four faces.

(In many other *Puranas*, there is no mention of Kalabhairava. Shiva performed the chopping off himself.)

Brahma died as soon as his head had been cut off. Shiva did manage to revive him. But the mere fact that Shiva had killed Brahma, meant that Shiva had committed the sin of killing a *brahmana*. As a result of this sin, Brahma's severed head got stuck to Kalabhairava's palm and would not be dislodged. (In accounts where Shiva was himself responsible for the killing, the severed head adhered to Shiva's palm.)

Kalabhairava roamed around the world and the head accompanied him on his travels. For a thousand years of the gods, Kalabhairava continued to travel. Eventually, Vishnu advised Kalabhairava to go to the sacred city of Varanasi.

As soon as Kalabhairava arrived at the city of Varanasi, the head *(kapala)* got dislodged *(mochana)*. A *tirtha* is a place of pilgrimage. The exact spot where this wonderful happening took place is accordingly known as *kapalamochana tirtha*.

There are many other *tirthas* that the *Kurma Purana* describes. Among these are Prayaga, Kurukshetra, Gaya and Madhuvana (Mathura). The glories of the river Narmada are also described. The waters of the river Sarasvati purify a sinner after three days of bathing, while the waters of the river Yamuna takes an entire week. The mere touch of a drop of water from the river Ganga purifies a sinner. But as for the river Narmada, the sight of the waters alone is enough.

## Nandi

There used to be a sage named Shilada. He was righteous and learned in the *shastras*.

To obtain a son, Shilada began to pray to Shiva. The *tapasya* went on for a thousand years and shiva appeared before Shilada.

"I am pleased with your meditation," said Shiva. "What boon do you desire?"

"Please grant me the boon that I may obtain a son who will not be born from a mother," replied Shilada. "And my son should be immortal."

Shiva granted the desired boon.

When Shilada was ploughing the land, a handsome boy suddenly appeared on the top of his plough. The four directions shone with the boy's radiance and the boy began to address Shilada as "father."

The son studied the *shastras* and became learned. He was given the name of Nandi.

Nandi wished to see Shiva and he also wished to become immortal. He therefore went to the shores of the ocean and started to pray to Shiva. He chanted the required *mantra* one crore times.

When Shiva appeared and wished to grant a boon, Nandi said, "Please grant me enough of life so that I can chant the *mantra* one crore times more."

Shiva appeared once again, and Nandi desired the same boon.

When this had happened three times, Shiva said, "Enough is enough. There is no need for any more chanting of incantations. I make you immortal. I also make you a *ganapati*, lord over the *ganas*. You will be my constant companion."

The place where Nandi chanted the incantation has become famous as *japyeshvara tirtha*.

The *maruts* had a daughter named Suyasha. Shiva himself arranged that Nandi should be married to Suyasha.

## Epilogue

Vishnu completed his recital of the *Kurma Purana* and the sages saluted him. They sung his praise.

The *Kurma Purana* is most sacred. A person who reads it attains Brahmaloka. A person who reads only one chapter of the text is forgiven all his sins. Undying *punya* is attained by an individual who donates this *Purana* to *brahmanas* in the months of Vaishakha or Kartika. Particularly sacred is the part that is known as the *brahmi samhita*.

But the text should never be read or recited in the presence of *shudras*. A person who ignores this injunction will surely go to hell. There is also a similar injunction about reciting the text to those who are disbelievers (that is, those who do not believe in the *Vedas*). A person who violates this injunction will be born as a dog in his next life.

You will almost certainly not be interested in donating the *Kurma Purana* to *brahmanas* in the months of Vaishakha or Kartika. But I hope you have found the stories interesting enough for you to wish to read the text in the original.

# Glossary

**adbhuta rasa:** literary sentiment of the strange or the miraculous

**adharma:** evil or irreligious, negation of dharma or righteousness

**adhyaya:** chapter

**Aditi:** Daksha's daughter, Kashyapa's wife, mother of the gods

**Adityas:** gods, sons of Aditi, believed to be twelve in number

**advaita brahmajnana:** knowledge of the union of the atman with the brahman

**agni:** fire, also the god of fire

**Agni Purana:** the eighth major Purana, narrated by the god Agni

**Airavata:** mythical elephant, Indra's transport

**akshouhini:** unit of an army with 109,350 infantrymen, 65,610 horses, 21,870 elephants and 21,870 chariots

**Amaravati:** Indra's habitat, used loosely for heaven

**Ambika:** a goddess, also means mother

**amrita:** nectar or drink that confers immortality

**amsha:** part, section

**amukta:** weapons not released from the hand during fighting

**anda:** egg

**anguli:** a finger, unit of measurement

**apana:** a form of breath

**apsara:** dancer or courtesan of heaven, used only in the feminine gender

**arthashastra:** political economy

**asana:** a seat, a posture of yoga

**ashrama:** hermitage, also stage in life

**ashvamedha:** a royal ceremony in which a horse is sacrificed after the king has conquered several countries

**Ashvinis:** two twin gods, also a nakshatra

**asura:** demon, used in the sense of negation of sura or god, used synonymously with danava or daitya

**Atharva Veda:** the fourth Veda

**atman:** the soul, the indestructible essence of life

**avatara:** incarnation, ten of Vishnu's in number

**ayana:** resting place, also a period of six months

**ayurveda:** the science of medicine

**Baladeva:** Krishna's elder brother

**Balarama:** See Baladeva

**Bhagavata Purana:** the fifth of the major Puranas, also known as Srimadbhagavata

**bhakti:** devotion or faith

**Bhargavas:** descendants of Bhrigu, a line of brahmana sages

**Bhavishya Purana:** the ninth of the major Puranas

**bhayanaka rasa:** literary sentiment pertaining to the horrible

**bheda:** the art of creating dissension amongst opposing parties, used by a king to rule

*bhuloka:* the earth, one of the three worlds

*bhuvana:* the universe, the world

*bhuvarloka:* a world that is above the earth but below heaven, one of the three worlds

*Brahma:* one of the Hindu Trinity of gods, the creator

*Brahma Purana:* the first of the major Puranas

*brahmacharya:* stage in life identified with celibacy and studenthood

*brahmajnana:* knowledge of the brahman

*brahman:* divine essence regarded as the cause of the universe

*brahmana:* one of the four castes, the duties of a brahmana being primarily to pray and perform ceremonies

*brahmanda:* the original egg from which the universe emerged

*Brahmanda Purana:* the eighteenth of the major Puranas

*brahmarshi:* type of sage

*brahmastra:* a divine weapon associated with Brahma

*Brahmavaivarta Purana:* the tenth of the major Puranas

*chakra:* circle, circular-bladed weapon used by Vishnu and Krishna

*Chamunda:* goddess, form of Durga

*chandala:* a man of low caste, an outcast, given the job of executioner

*Chandi:* the goddess Durga

*Chandi:* a text popular in eastern India glorifying the goddess Durga, chapters 81 to 93 of the Markandeya Purana

*Chandra:* the moon, the moon-god

*Chandra vamsha:* the lunar dynasty

*chhanda:* metre

*daityas:* demons, sons of Diti, used synonymously with danavas and asuras

*Daksha:* Brahma's son, one of the ten prajapatis or rulers

*dakshina:* fee, payment made to a teacher

*Damodara:* Krishna's name, literally one whose stomach is tied with a rope

*dana:* donation of alms, used by a king to rule

*danavas:* demons, sons of Danu, used synonymously with daityas and asuras

*danda:* punishment, used by a king to rule, stick, Yama's weapon

*devarshi:* type of sage

*devas:* gods, literally those with shining bodies

*dhanurdanda:* length of a bow, unit of measurement

*dhanurveda:* a text on weapons and armaments

*dhanusha:* bow

*Dhanvantari:* the physician of the gods, emerged from the churning of the ocean

*dharma:* righteousness, good, the god of dharma being Yama

*dharmashastras:* sacred texts, often theological

*Dhruvaloka:* a world above the constellation of the Great Bear, the habitation of Dhruva

*dhuli:* unit of measurement

*dhyana:* meditation

*Diti:* daughter of Daksha, wife of Kashyapa, mother of the demons or daityas

***dronimukha:*** type of habitation

***dvapara:*** the third of the four eras or yugas, consisting of two thousand years of the gods

***dvipas:*** the seven regions into which the earth is divided

***gada:*** mace

***gadya:*** prose

***ganadevata:*** common gods

***gandharva:*** singers or minstrels of heaven

***garhasthya:*** stage of life when one is a householder

***Garuda:*** a mythical bird which was Vishnu's transport

***Garuda Purana:*** mahapurana, seventeenth in the list of major Puranas

***gayatri:*** name of an incantation or mantra, also a goddess

***ghosha:*** type of habitation where cowherds live

***Gita:*** Krishna's teachings to Arjuna on the eve of the Kuruk-shetra war, eighteenth chapter of Bhishma Parvan of the Mahabharata, also known as Shrimadbhagavadgita

***govyuti:*** unit of measurement

***grama:*** type of habitation where shudras live

***guna:*** elemental quality, three in number

***guru:*** teacher, preceptor

***hasta:*** unit of measurement

***hasya rasa:*** literary sentiment of humour

***Indra:*** title of King of the gods, title changes hands from manvantara to manvantara, presently held by Purandara

***indrajala:*** jugglery or balancing act amongst opposing parties, used by a king to rule

***ishana:*** name of kalpa or cycle

***japa:*** ceaseless repetition of an incantation

***jatismara:*** one who remembers earlier births

***jaya:*** victory, name of a goddess who is a companion of Parvati

***jivatman:*** the soul or atman that is in living bodies

***jnana:*** knowledge

***jnana yoga:*** yoga attained through pursuing knowledge

***kaivalya:*** absorption into the divine essence through knowledge

***Kala:*** unit of time, also the god of Death

***Kali:*** the last of the four yugas or eras, consisting of one thousand years of the gods, also the name of a gandharva

***kali:*** goddess who emerged from Ambika's forehead

***kalika:*** goddess Parvati after Koushiki or Ambika emerged from Parvati's cells; a dark-hued goddess

***Kalki:*** the tenth and last of Vishnu's avataras, yet to come

***kalpa:*** a cycle of time consisting of fourteen manvantaras

***kalpavriksha:*** mythical tree which yielded whatever one wanted

***karma yoga:*** yoga achieved through actions or work

***Kartikeya:*** god of war, also known as Skanda, son of Shiva and Parvati

*karuna rasa:* literary sentiment of pathos

*karvataka:* fortress-like habitation

*kashtha:* unit of time

*kavandha:* headless

*keshagra:* very small unit of measurement

*khetaka:* stick, also fortress-like habitation

*kirata:* a hunter

*kosha:* cell

*Koumari:* goddess created from Kartikeya's body

*Koushiki:* goddess Ambika who emerged from Parvati's cells

*Krishna:* the eighth avatara of Vishnu, son of Vasudeva and Devaki

*Krishna Dvaipayana Vedavyasa:* son of Parashara, believed to be the composer of the Mahabharata and the Puranas

*krishnapaksha:* fortnight in which the moon wanes

*krita:* the first of the four yugas or eras, consisting of four thousand years of the gods, also known as satya yuga

*kshatriya:* class whose duty is was to take up arms and protect the world

*kubera:* god of wealth, treasurer of the gods

*kumbhaka:* process of controlling one's breath in yoga

*Kurma:* turtle, second avatara of Vishnu

*Kurma Purana:* the fifteenth in the list of major Puranas

*Kurukshetra:* plain in North India named after Kuru, where the war between the Kauravas and the Pandavas was fought

*lakshanas:* characteristics, any Purana must satisfy five of these

*Lakshmi:* goddess of wealth and prosperity, emerged from the churning of the ocean

*linga:* Shiva's image

*Linga Purana:* mahapurana, the eleventh major Purana

*loka:* a region

*Madana:* god of love

*magadha:* attendants of king who chanted his praise

*Mahabharata:* sacred epic composed by Vyasadeva, containing one lakh shlokas

*Mahadeva:* name for Shiva

*Mahamaya:* goddess of illusions

*mahapurana:* major Purana, eighteen in number, all believed to have been composed by Vyasadeva

*mahisha:* buffalo

*Mahishasura:* a demon

*manava:* human being, descendant of Manu

*mantra:* prayer or incantation, usually secret

*Manu:* ruler of a manvantara or era, fourteen in number, all deriving their name from the first one.

*manvantara:* an era that the earth passes through, there are fourteen of these in any cycle

*Markandeya Purana:* mahapurana, seventh in the list of major Puranas

*marut:* gods of wind, companions of Indra, seven or forty-nine in number

*matsya:* fish, first avatara of Vishnu

*Matsya Purana:* the sixteenth major Purana

*maya:* illusion or hallucination

*Mayamoha:* being created by Vishnu out of his own body

*mimamsa:* form of knowledge, philosophy

*moksha:* final salvation

*muhurta:* unit of time

*naga:* snake or tribe which used snakes as totems

*nakshatra:* star, twenty-seven in number

*nandana kanana:* garden of pleasure, located in heaven

*Narada Purana:* the sixth major Purana

*naraka:* hell, several in number

*narasimha:* half-man and half-lion, fourth avatara of Vishnu

*nimesha:* unit of measuring time

*nishada:* tribe of hunters living in the Vindhyas

*nishka:* unit of measurement

*nyaya:* form of knowledge

*om:* sacred word, the root of mantras in the Vedas

*oshadi:* medicinal herbs

*outtama:* third manvantara, named after King Outtama

*pada:* unit of measurement

*Padma Purana:* the second major Purana

*padmasana:* lotus-like seating posture of yoga

*padya:* poetry

*paishacha:* form of marriage

*paksha:* half of month, the lunar fortnight, side or party

*panchajanya:* name of Krishna's conch-shell

*pani:* hand

*pani-mukta:* weapon hurled from the hand

*papa:* sins, evil deeds

*paramanu:* smallest unit of measurement

*paramatman:* all-pervading supreme soul or brahman  Vishnu

*parashu:* axe

*Parashurama:* destroyer of kshatriyas, sixth incarnation of Vishnu

*parijata:* a heavenly flower, emerged from the churning of the ocean

*Parvati:* goddess, daughter of the Himalaya mountains

*pasha:* noose, Varuna's weapon

*patala:* underworld, seven in number

*pativrata:* woman devoted to her husband

*pitri:* ancestors in heaven

*prakriti:* perfect balance of the three basic gunas or characteristics

*pralaya:* destruction, upheaval

*prana vayu:* breath of life

**pranayama:** technique of meditation by controlling one's breath

**pratisarga:** section in the Puranas which describes periodic creations and destructions

**prayashchitta:** atonement or penance for sins

**Prithivi:** the earth, named after King Prithu

**puja:** worship or prayer

**punya:** store of merit earned through good deeds

**pura:** fortress-like habitation

**puraka:** a process of yoga to control inhalation

**Purana:** sacred and ancient text, eighteen major (maha-puranas) and eighteen minor (upapuranas) in number

**Purana Samhita:** the original text of the Puranas

**raja dharma:** code of duties for a king

**rajarshi:** type of sage

**rajas:** the guna or quality of passion

**rajasika Purana:** Purana that emphasises creation and Brahma

**rajasuya yajna:** royal sacrificial ceremony when a king tries to conquer other kingdoms

**rakshasa:** demon, originated from the water

**rakshasa vivaha:** form of marriage

**Rama:** seventh avatara of Vishnu

**rasa:** literary sentiment, nine in number

**rechaka:** process of yoga to control exhalation

**Rig:** incantation, the first of the four Vedas

**rishi:** sage, hermit

**roudra rasa:** literary sentiment of wrath and awe

**Rudra:** god, Brahma's son, another name for Shiva

**sabha:** assembly

**sama:** technique of appeasement, used by a king to rule

**Sama Veda:** third of the four Vedas

**samadhi:** deep and intense state of meditation

**samasa:** rule of grammar for forming compound words

**samudra-manthana:** churning of the ocean

**sandhi:** rule of grammar for forming compound word

**sandhya:** evening, period between two yugas

**sandhyamsha:** period between two yugas

**sannyasa:** the final stage of life, hermithood

**saptarshi:** seven major rishis, changing from one manvantara to another, Great Bear constellation

**Sarasvati:** name of a river, goddess of learning

**sarga:** section in Purana describing creation

**sarovara:** lake

**sarpa:** snake

**sattva:** the guna or quality of goodness

**sattvika Purana:** Purana exalting Vishnu and emphasising devotion and faith

*satya:* truth, the first of the four eras or yugas, also known as krita yuga, consisting of four thousand years of the gods

*Savita:* god sometimes identified with the sun-god

*Shachi:* Indra's wife

*shakhanagar:* habitation, cantonment

*shakti:* spear, also a goddess

*shanta rasa:* literary sentiment of placidity

*shastra:* holy text

*Shesha:* great snake of the underworld

*shishya:* student, disciple

*Shiva:* god, Mahadeva

*Shiva Purana:* the eleventh major Purana

*shloka:* couplet, verse

*shmashana:* cremation-ground

*shraddha:* funeral ceremony

*shringara rasa:* literary sentiment associated with love

*shrutis:* sacred texts

*shudra:* the lowest of the four classes, their duties being to serve the other three classes

*shuklapaksha:* fortnight in which the moon waxes

*Skanda:* Kartikeya

*Skanda Purana:* the thirteenth major Purana

*soma:* herbal drink

*songhasha:* habitation

*sudarshana chakra:* name of the bladed discus used by Vishnu and Krishna

*sura:* god

*Surya:* sun-god, sun

*Surya Vamsha:* solar dynasty

*suta:* royal attendant who chanted the king's praise, born of a brahmana mother and kshatriya father

*svarga:* heaven

*svarloka:* heaven

*svayamvara:* ceremony at which a bride choses her husband from several suitors

*syamantaka:* name of a jewel

*Taittiriya:* branch of Yajur Veda named after the bird tittira

*tamas:* quality associated with darkness

*tamasika Purana:* Purana exalting Shiva and rituals and norms

*tapasya:* long-term meditation under some form of hardship

*tirtha:* place of piligrimage

*tithi:* lunar day

*trasarenu:* unit of measurement

*treta yuga:* second of the four yugas, consisting of three thousand years of the gods

*trishula:* trident, three-pronged spear

*tvashtra.* divine weapon

*Upanishads:* sacred texts

*upapurana:* minor Purana, eighteen in number

*upavita:* the sacred thread that is the mark of the first three classes

*upeksha:* ignoring, used by a king to rule

*vajra:* Indra's weapon; identified as a club; also thunder

*vamana:* dwarf, fifth incarnation of Vishnu

*vamsha:* dynasty, genealogy

*vamshanucharita:* history of royal dynasties

*vana:* arrow

*vanaprastha:* forest-dwelling stage

*varaha:* boar, third incarnation of Vishnu

*varna:* caste or social class, also letter of alphabet or complexion

*varsha:* geographical region

*Vedas:* sacred texts

*Vedavyasa:* composer of the Mahabharata and the Puranas

*vidya:* knowledge

*vidyadhara:* singer of heaven

*vimana:* space vehicle

*Vishvadevas:* gods

*vishvarupa:* Vishnu's universal form

*vitasti:* unit of measurement

*vrata:* religious rite

*yajna:* prayer ceremony presided over by some sage where a sacrifice or
    offering is made in the presence of a holy fire and amidst chantings of holy
    texts

*Yajur Veda:* one of the four Vedas

*yaksha:* demi-god, companion of Kubera

*Yama:* god of Death

*yamaduta:* servant of Yama

*yantra:* machine

*yantramukta:* weapons launched from a machine

*yava:* unit of measurement

*yoga:* meditation that seeks to bring about union between the human soul and
    the divine essence

*yogi:* one who performs yoga

*yojana:* unit of measurement

*yuka:* unit of measurement